THE
LIFE
EXCHANGER

By: Brian Irwin

Author and excellent teacher on relationships from his first book
CONNECTED HEARTS

The Life Exchanger
by Brian Irwin

Printed in the United States of America

ISBN 9781609577681

The Life Exchanger allegory is a work of fiction. All the characters, events, places, and dialogue are completely of the author's creative imagination and are not to be misconstrued or read-between-the-lines with hidden agendas targeted toward anyone or any group. Any resemblance to actual people, events, places, or groups is purely a matter of concepts by association to things that may have similarities, but without motive or intent.

New Beginnings Coaching & Counseling
6612 East Dick Ford Lane
Knoxville, TN. 37920
Office: (865) 609-8777
brianirwin@comcast.net
www.thelifeexchanger.com
www.exchangedforlife.com

www.xulonpress.com

Contents

Preface .... *ix*

Chapter 1   **A Common Survivors Story** 15

Chapter 2   **Waking up to a Big Dream** 42

Chapter 3   **Identity, "Who Am I?"** 58

Chapter 4   **From Brokenness To Wholeness** 78

Chapter 5   **Overcoming The Illusion Of Light** 103

Chapter 6   **The Crazy-Makers** 126

Chapter 7   **Finding the Path Through the Forbidden Forest** 143

Chapter 8   **The Language of the Innermost Being** 161

Chapter 9   **Facing The Terrifying Creatures** 181

Chapter 10   **Building Community With Other Believers** 215

This book is for Commoners who want more out of relationships
Than surviving rejection. To all those who are tired of
Coping mechanisms just getting them by for
Another day of the same old routine.

§

I dedicate this project to the inspiration of my children:
Shawn and his new wife Rachael, and Aubri and her
New husband Anthony ("Tony") Beard.

To the commitment of the home group of believers Sherri
And I have been fellowshipping with for the past year:
The DeToro's, the Cline's, the Monday's, and Mitzi.
Their hearts have completely embraced
The Exchanged For Life principles.

Most of all, I wish to acknowledge The Life Exchanger Himself.
Without His amazing grace and love, none of us would
Know our Inner Longings for a Big Dream to
Exchange our old identity for Royalty.

Preface

"...what can a man give in <u>exchange</u> for his soul?"

A re you a *survivor* who believes every human being on earth has a nagging itch somewhere deep inside to be a *thriver* ...wanting to exchange their common life for royalty? If so, what would you expect in return?

The answer might surprise you.

Back in 1981, a Commoner in the United Kingdom rose to global notoriety from the announcement of her engagement to royalty. This young lady born into an old, aristocratic English family exchanged her former identity for royal connections. Who am I speaking of?... Lady Diana, Princess of Wales, (Diana Spencer; July 1, 1961 – August 31, 1997). This popular international media icon of the late 20th century captured my attention along with a global audience of over 750 million people on her wedding day. I was captivated by her story as an example of an exchanged identity. Only, her story had a tragic ending.

However, there is a greater exchange offered by the Life Exchanger to every common person for the highest status of royalty in the *Heavenly* Kingdom for *happily ever after*.

No matter where I've traveled in North America, whether among hardworking volunteers of Knoxville or hard-charging city-folk of Nashville, Atlanta, Dallas, St. Louis, Chicago, Canada and beyond, I've met a lot of interesting people with a variety of philosophies and beliefs. The irony of what everyone has in common?... I have yet to find one person who didn't desire a good return on their life investments. Some may not be able to express it. Others may have forgotten it. And some may have quit believing in it.

But it's there.

Commonly speaking, we all have a nagging itch for more meaning and purpose in these things we call our hearts.

I call these global hardcore naggings "Inner Longings." Like DNA woven throughout every fiber of our being, our Inner Longings permeate the very depth of our heart; even to dividing between soul and spirit. Only, millions of Commoners are left without a clue about how to live their royal destiny on this side of Heaven.

Ironically, this happens for a reason: to motivate you to continue pursuing the kind of life you were born to live, spiritually! In fact, everyone's been given an invitation to experience the greatest exchange on earth! And yet, on your quest to champion your Inner Longings, I'm offering you an animated version of what I've learned on my own personal journey intended to help empower your unique identity to come alive. If you accept the challenge, in return, your passions will find fulfillment through being Exchanged For Life—from a survivor to a thriver, and from a Commoner to Royalty!

Consider this: on a quest for more, we will walk through some powerful and significant principles showing you how to live the Abundant, Victorious, Royal life. Understanding who you are (which affects your everyday choices) takes you to a deeper place you may not have ever discovered before, especially in relationships. Take a dive plunging heart first into the deep end of the freedom pool from fear, shame, guilt, pain, and rejection. There, you will learn how the Life Exchanger lives *through* you, the good work He begins *in* you, for heart-connections.

Welcome to my book, *The Life Exchanger*, a practical strategy for getting the greatest return on your relationship investments with your Creator and others.

The Life Exchanger is an allegory. This is the story of Elton, a Commoner with a survivor's mentality who leaves the land of Suburb of Soul to pursue the Great Exchange in the HeartLand. This story will introduce you to your very own unique meaning and purpose I want to help mentor you through... connecting your thoughts and feelings with your heart in your significant relationships.

I will serve as your Connector, using techniques I've learned along my own personal journey in Life-Coaching and Discipleship-Counseling. This Inside-out approach empowers and motivates you to champion your journey in search for more. Each step outlined in the following chapters is designed to compel you toward becoming more like the divine Mediator walking by grace through faith in the Spirit.

If you're like me, we can all use some help discovering what the Grace-walk looks like. Along life's journey there are unforgettable illustrations capturing the essence of grace for real heart-connections. From the greatest epic story ever told—out of Egypt through the Wilderness into the Promise-land—we've come to appreciate how love compelled a story where an ancient Middle-Eastern nation collided with surrounding nations before ever completing their destiny. Like them, we all have an eternal destiny for royalty by the grace of God. Consequently, despite all the trial and error, the Life Exchanger still requires something better than going through "performance-based" motions, He demands a *heart exchange*. In this allegory, it's not merely a unique tale about ordinary survivors caught up in life's web of struggles. No. This is a story single-handedly aligning our perspectives in search of that hard to find balance between spirit and soul spoken of in the greatest Manual For Life ever written, the Bible.

In choosing an allegory, like parables, it helps illustrate a point by simply using metaphors and word-pictures. This method follows a long line of masterful mediators who've used storytelling as an effective method for their craft. Hannah

Hurnard and *Hinds' Feet On High Places*, for example. Or C.S. Lewis and *The Chronicles of Narnia*. And more recent, Bruce Wilkinson and *The Dream Giver*, to mention a few. Mediating between the divine and man has been part of covenant relationships ever since the Creator walked in the cool of the Garden with the first human beings. Incarnate, the most effective Mediator in history walked the earth over two thousand years ago teaching His disciples through parables expressing spiritual truths about relationships. By His example, using word-pictures might be the most efficient teaching tool ever used regarding our need for heart connections.

So imagine through your relational-lens your own Inner Longings for more meaning and purpose beyond the surface. That's right! ...beyond the two-dimensional realm of your soul and body. You know, all that mental stress, emotional roller-coaster ride, and weak-willed behavior psychologists attempt to remedy through *cognitive-behavioral modification.*

Instead, picture a dispelling tale showcased in a quaint little town called Suburb of Soul (near an oasis, if you will) with a deep well of hope in an Eden-like garden; a place called the HeartLand. Thirsty, like a summer drought, passions of the heart are drawn to a pool full of dreams and aspirations. Elton, a survivor in need of unlearning his bad habits, learns to live according to his intended birthright. Gifts, personality, and talents all come alive as if for the very first time! There are no more islands for misfit toys. No more disabling fear paralyzing love's desire to come out of his comfort zone! Instead, Elton discovers there is a kind of freedom from the need to be in control—enabling relationships to connect with his heart.

Although *The Life Exchanger* is about seeking a kind of investment conventional wisdom knows nothing about, in the end, each courageous sojourner must open his/her heart to something called the *Fair Exchange*. Don't buy into the plastic ideas or vain philosophies declaring men and women are from other planets. For this reason, we will peer into a quest here on earth processing thoughts and emotions with our heart, by keeping a personal Journey Journal at the end of each chapter.

Finally, like with Elton, a new found freedom liberates us *from* the faulty system, *to* the life we've always dreamed of! Through endearing affections designed to dive into the deeper end of the relational pool, Elton comes to a place where he finally interacts on an intimate level with his heart. Whether for a healthier new relationship or simply a better quality of life, he learns how to make heart connections like never before. While discovering the truth about tri-part beings, he taps into a third-dimension where truths are embraced from the Manual For Life regarding his spirit, soul, and body.

Oh, and one more thing... as he takes that big leap of faith on an adventure for a lifetime, destiny would have Elton's quest find a spiritual knowledge and wisdom in the Manual For Life hidden from the mere mind. Amazing for a man, his journey is about to reveal the answers to questions like: what is "True Identity"?, what is "true grace"?, what is "unconditional love"?, what is the need for "accountability in community"?, what are "soulish behaviors"?, what is the "Innermost Being"?, what is the difference between "soul and spirit"?, and what are "heart-connected" relationships in the "Fair Exchange"?

Although he was forewarned, '*it's impossible to teach someone something they think they already know,*' unmistakably, Elton had to destroy the man he was becoming in order to become the man he was always meant to be.

Remember, if you want a good return on your life investment, it's only when you learn to abide in the truth with your heart, that the truth makes you free in your life!

Faithfully,

Brian E. Irwin

Chapter 1

A Common Survivors Story

⌐———⌐

In a time not so long ago, at a place not so far away, a young man named Elton with a Scots-Irish heritage lived among Commoners just outside the big metropolis in a town called Suburb of Soul.

As most days were like other days, Elton was an ordinary Commoner who went to his normal job on the weekdays, relaxed on the weekends, and worshiped at the Local Gathering on Sunday. After work, Elton, who was usually full of his *Self*, filled his belly with soul food much like he did the day before. Then he sat in his high-back leather swivel chair, pushing and clicking a mouse fixated on a box. When bored with that box, he'd recline in his lounger staring at another box that fascinated most Commoners for hours at a time.

Sometimes, his girlfriend, Elaine, came over after connecting online or by texting, only to sit and stare at a box together. Sometimes, they played games and music on a box. Sometimes, they even met at a sports bar to watch their home team on a box. And other times, Elton would go over to his parents to watch a box where he first learned this habitual pastime.

For the most part, this young survivor loved life as it was, with all his soul. As a cleaver thinker, he thought he was sufficiently satisfied with his Self-accomplishments through music and soccer and chasing girls. As one who liked planning on dependable things, he accepted his routine as normal under the current status quo, as long as he could be independent and Self-sufficient. But mostly, he was content with what he had. At least… with what he was conditioned to think he had.

Remarkably, even though this happy-go-lucky dreamer had all the normal qualities of a typical male, he was about to learn something quite spectacular for his half of the human race. Strangely, Elton was bothered by something nagging his insides beneath his soul. It was a mysterious urge determined to connect his identity at a deeper level with his heart. But, in his logical thinking mind, he had no idea where this urge was coming from. No one in Suburb of Soul told him he was supposed to connect his identity with his heart, especially when most Commoners were encouraged to build a wall of protection around their heart's identity from rejection. Normally, in Suburb of Soul, identity was based on what you do, in order to know who you are. No one could afford to be vulnerable with their heart if they wanted acceptance for their soul.

Contrary to *Self-help* specialists among those known around town as Pselfologists, some Commoners took a risk. Subconsciously, Elton was a risk-taker. He daydreamed about other options unlike the common scientific approaches he learned in Pselfology. But that's all they were… silly dreams.

And yet, he was about to find himself on a quest where Self had to unlearn most things he'd ever learned or dreamed.

Nevertheless, in his macho, good-Ole-boy mentality from an Old-School upbringing, Elton thought he found the answer. Like so many other young men, the answer to his lonely dilemma was found in a compliant, sweet southern bell — with stunning good looks to match. "A trophy girl"—that was the answer. They'd eventually get married and learn to never ask the uncommon question among most Commoners …"how the heck was a surviving man and a surviving woman supposed to connect with their hearts… for a lifetime?"

Most just learned to survive anyway.

Reality usually sets in like a lead balloon; inevitably unrealistic expectations collide in midair, and then take a nosedive for the disaster zone. Having come from a dysfunctional background, wisely, he sought counsel before impact. But not just any counsel. He sought the counsel of a Connector. Elton desperately wanted to know how in the world he and his future bride were ever going to make a life together under such extreme differences. It seemed almost impossible *not* to repeat the patterns of the previous generations. So, like everyone else he knew, this partnership destined for disaster needed more than just a little help ... it needed an extreme makeover!

"What in the world did that look like?" Elton wondered. Encouragingly, a divine invitation was delivered in the midst of his sublime situation. But, I'm getting way ahead of myself. I need to take you back to the beginning of how Elton discovered the *Great Exchange* with the Life Exchanger before he ever embraced the *Fair Exchange* with his soul mate, Elaine.

~

Living in the quaint little town of Suburb of Soul, tucked away in the mountains, ordinary people accepted their status as Commoners, especially hardy Scots-Irish like Elton with a mix of Venezuelan in his blood. Unpopular among his family and peers, not knowing it, Elton was about to set out on an adventure far away from his comfort zone. Only, his comfort zone was located at his Perspective Home in a river-town flowing with relative values and beliefs passed down from generation to generation. Different from his normal thoughts and emotions for the soul, Elton was about to find himself searching for hope in a place called the HeartLand, located somewhere in the forbidden, majestic Misty Mountains. It was forbidden because this was a mysterious place to those who lived according to their souls. It was majestic because of the breathtaking vistas clearing the clouds looking up toward the heavens. Yet, the HeartLand has a hopeful flavor of peace and freedom for any Seeker in search of becoming a Thriver with their spirit. However, each Commoner could only come by invitation. If anyone took the risk, they would experience the ultimate heart-connection. But, this was a very dangerous pursuit without a Connector. Many have tied to go it alone, but failed, and returned hard-hearted.

Ironically, Elton was blessed to have known an old friend of the family named Kindred-Spirit—a very humble yet complex Connector who spent time with Elton most times he was in town. In fine fashion, there was one detailed account during his young adult years when he was challenged by his Connector to become a Thriver, a true follower of Mediator.

"Great to see you again, Kindred-Spirit," Elton said. "And hey, thanks for meeting me here at my favorite restaurant... Self-Serve Soul Food. If you don't mind, while we're waiting to order, I have a question for you."

"Sure, fire away," chuckled the older gentleman, a drip of soda trickling down his big grin.

Kindred-Spirit exchanged curious looks between him and his young survivor friend.

"Well, I've always wanted to know about something no one's willing to talk about," Elton began. "According to traditions, why are most Commoners labeled with soulish traits in Suburb of Soul?" asking directly his mentoring Connector without hesitation.

"Well my young friend," Kindred-Spirit looked paranoid to the left and to the right out of the corner of each eye, then, leaned forward over the table with a whispering voice, "listen, many millenniums ago, people began to identify more and more from an *outside-in* approach with their soulish traits—those thoughts and emotions governed by Self. You see, the need Self has in each Commoner, when independent from Mediator, is to be in control. But it's only an illusion of control. The Manual For Life urges us to recognize our Inner Longings for *real* joy from an *inside-out* perspective—where *Comforter* is in control..."

Kindred-Spirit continued in his usual lecturing way translating mysteries he had discovered. Not having but two children of his own, grown and gone for years, he loved sharing his research and wisdom with young adults like Elton.

Up until this point, throughout all his childhood years, without any explanations, Elton thought he lived in good faith worshipping at the Local Gathering. He always believed in The Life Exchanger, Mediator, Comforter, and of course, read from the Manual For Life. No one ever challenged his beliefs as long as he followed the normal routine. But now he opened a can of worms with Kindred-Spirit, rocking his world beyond comprehension.

With his seven awkward teenage years behind him, he confidently reached out to other Commoners on his terms during his college years, sharing his faith at Suburb of Soul University whenever it hit his fancy. Now in his twenties, at first, living single afforded him the luxury to have a more carefree lifestyle to climb the corporate performance-ladder along with the religious law-ladder; that was, until he and his china-cup dream girl, Elaine, clashed. She wanted a real man who would love her with all his heart.

The whispering continued across the table, "...normally stoic in adulthood, instead of open hearts maintaining the innocence of love and affection from childhood, most Commoners eventually built walls of protection keeping themselves safe from fear, shame, guilt, and pain, leading to rejection." Kindred-Spirit covered all his bases about the history of Suburb of Soul.

"I know you're trying to help me with good intensions, old man, but I need a translator to explain your explanations. I'm not getting the difference between soul and spirit and how to think and feel with my heart. Where did you come up with this stuff? And, can I just get something off my chest I've always been wondering? Your name. Why do people call you Kindred-Spirit? Heck, with all you've been through, I'm surprised they didn't nickname you Stoney or something like that." Frustration built a mask on his face as Elton needed help understanding.

Unannounced, keeping his curiosities a secret, there were urges stirring within Elton like never before. And now his Connector unleashed a possible explanation that would encounter mysteries in a world beyond what had become his comfort zone. It was no longer ok to simply believe in the same values normal to all Commoners at the Local Gathering. Elton and his significant other were about to discover a whole new world made for heart connections, separating them from friends and loved ones.

However, up until now, Suburb of Soul captivated Elton's world mainly concerning his Self-life. He hung out among a community of Commoners where two kinds of Self stood out the most: Justifying-Feelers and Rationalizing-Thinkers—in short, Feelers and Thinkers. Academically, he became leery of those from a more sophisticated menu who called themselves Intuitive-Feelers and Conscience-Thinkers—typically characterizing what was commonly referred to as traits of personality. According to the Pselfologists grand scientific discovery, these generic traits were located deep inside the limbic portion of the brain. They were recognized as each individual's identity. Incidentally, *"Soul"* was the accepted term in Suburb of Soul identifying each Commoner according to their unique personality traits (from the Latin that is).

In spite all the hoopla and big stink Pselfologists made over this so-called "Self-analysis discovery", many of the Local Gatherings taught values and beliefs from the Manual For Life liberally. For anyone who took the time to learn from this grand book of wisdom, he or she would know it simply dispelled any kind of "flesh modification." In fact, Elton discovered a different explanation of the soulish life. Perhaps it was due to something somewhere deep inside his tender heart nagging him there's more. He came to recognize there was something big missing deeper inside regarding his own basic understanding of life and death— those nagging Inner Longings kept itching somewhere in what he'd come to know as his Innermost Being.

Then, out of the cruel fate of intimacy with his future covenant bride, the most amazing thing happened. His Inner Longings discovered something radical called *Exchanged For Life* principles! Unbelievably, its original conception came from early Thrivers who taught the Exchanged For Life principles in a far eastern land. Consequently, Elton had to eventually discover his True Identity in the Mediator before ever embracing the heart of the doe of his youth—much different from his religious upbringing in the Local Gathering.

Awkwardly, his Connector knew he'd have to make an impeccable discovery about his heart while stumbling into young adulthood! No matter where Elton turned, personal relationships at the intimate level were ridiculously hard... at best! Despite the warnings of his Connector, everything else he'd been taught, always believed in, and tried to live by, didn't make a lick of sense. When it boiled down to his spiritual experience, a boatload of spiritual disciplines weighed him down like a backpack full of performance-based rules and regulations. He found himself getting worn out while trying to work out expectations of others.

Having his eyes fixed on a sweet southern bell, Elaine (eventually picking her to be his covenant bride), they would settle down. Only, there was no *settling* about it. There were times when these two sweethearts couldn't settle their differences about anything! Like their parents before them, one dominant personality with the other's compliance seemed to be the only lifeline keeping them together.

"And I'm here to tell you, if it's a natural thing when opposites attract (which I'm beginning to wonder), then it only stands to reason when extreme opposites retract, that's when one's whole world falls apart," Kindred-Spirit was on his soapbox.

Truth of the matter, that's exactly what Elton was about to experience... the collapse of a divided relationship.

Unfortunately, Elton somehow didn't quite grasp the meaning of that one key component for the longest time—the part about thinking and feeling with his heart. "What does that mean?" he wondered. Perhaps, like the evasive nature of unconditional love, so were the Exchanged For Life principles. No one but Kindred-Spirit had ever attempted to explain to him a solid working definition to something so subjective as the spiritual nature of the heart. Most summed it up as thoughts and feelings mixed in with some religious moral principles, while others implied that soul and spirit are simply synonymous terms, meaning the same thing about the immaterial part of people. He didn't know how he would ever understand the protective wall around his elusive heart in a world that watered down the issues?

"Like the calloused hands from fields for plowing," Kindred-Spirit said as he stretched out his thick palms and protruding sausage fingers, "so do hearts subtly harden over the course of years from difficult relationships."

"I just don't understand," the young survivor whimpered.

Unbeknownst to Elton, he'd been relying on his soulish thoughts and emotions for so long to find favor in the Life Exchanger's graces, that he lost his first love in all the wrong places. In fact, it seemed as though a closet rebellious Yankee, he was simply expected by all the other Commoners to conform and comply to written and unwritten rules according to good-Ole-boy mentalities ...well, that was if he wanted acceptance among the community of other Commoners. On top of all that confusion, the gold and silver glitter of wisdom and understanding lost their luster as the Manual For Life became a burden to bear.

Funny, as an expert in surveying and infrastructure, in the subculture plumb bob of the Local Gatherings social structure, with a benchmark centered on family and friends, acceptance was just as performance-based as anywhere else. Regrettably, he kept getting into train wrecks, one right after the other—the worse had always been with the opposite sex.

"Yeah, but I feel—" Elton tried to finally get a thought in but his words were cut short by the abruptness.

"—It isn't about beginning with emotional feelings," said Kindred-Spirit quickly interrupting, "which are part of the soul. As a matter of fact, my young friend, most Commoners are missing the deeper abiding *peace* which surpasses each person's understanding. You see, Elton, things don't always appear to make sense in our natural mind and emotions even though they are very real to our spirit. That's why becoming a true follower is hard to come by unless there's a nagging urge for an *exchange* of the heart, which bears a burden in every true believers new nature."

Elton, who was on the edge of his seat with excitement to share, leaned into the face of his Connector.

"Yeah... listen, old man," he barked back, then leaned back in his seat, scattered like ADHD, acting as if not hearing a word Kindred-Spirit said, "I can't stand feeling unappreciated and misunderstood. Ya know what I'm saying, Kindred-Spirit? Oh, and another thing, I've been bothered lately by this nagging urge to some day go outside the normal cultural boundaries of Suburb of Soul in order to become a follower of Mediator, and find more meaning and purpose out there. You know... that thing I've heard you talk about... my Inner Longings. But my parents have told me it's too dangerous. They've consistently told me that our Creator only helps those who work hard with their body and soul."

With a short look of "I just said that" on his face, Kindred-Spirit shook off the distraction.

"So, do you believe that philosophy in life?" Kindred-Spirit asked irritably.

The effect of the sarcastic tone scrambled the thoughts in Elton's brain.

"Yeah. I do... I think? I mean... well, you see, the whole looking out for number one by building a wall of protection around my heart from all the fear, shame, guilt, and pain associated with rejection, is the part that really confuses me. Call me crazy, but I'm not afraid of no spooky freak like Rejector. From my perspective, keeping a wall of protection around my heart seems Self defeating? Kinda like when I played soccer. Remember the year I nearly broke my ankle? I wore a cast for healing. But then I tried to wear it a little longer for protection from getting injured again. Heck, I even thought about putting one on my other ankle,"

Elton said with his own playful flavor of sarcasm, then made a profound point. "As you can imagine, it completely hindered me from playing up to my fullest potential. Isn't it the same thing if we build a protective wall around our heart? Why would Commoners do that?"

"NOT ONLY THAT," Kindred-Spirit thundered, while leaning back in his chair, then taking another sip from his coke, "Due to these infamous walls of protection built between the soul and spirit, our soulish desires commonly build walls. These walls? They're not only to *guard* our heart... but they make us feel like we're in *control*. In fact, that keeps the most important relationship *need* we have deep inside our spirit from fulfilling our desire to become Thrivers. If you've ever noticed, Elton, the Manual For Life commonly refers to a follower's spiritual heart as the Innermost Being. Ironically, we shouldn't build a wall around that part of us where Mediator lives in and *through* us, right? When we build a wall around our heart, we keep Him inside from doing what He wants to accomplish on the outside."

With a perplexing look on his face, Elton barked back another rebuttal pounding the table with his fist.

"Right, but come on, man, we're talking about all-knowing, all-powerful divine Mediator. How in the world can we do anything to prevent Him from doing His will *through* us? And another thing... how do you know we can build a wall around Him?"

Elton stared at the red-faced Connector, while glancing at their pale-faced waitress standing patiently waiting for orders off the menu.

After they ordered, Kindred-Spirit and Elton both regained their composures. Kindred-Spirit shared his thoughts like a winded bullfrog and watching Elton closely not to interrupt again.

"All right. Remember what Mediator told His followers in the Manual For Life?" Connector said. *"I stand at the door and knock, if any Commoner hears my voice and opens the door, I will come into them and dine with them."* You see

Elton, Mediator won't be able to live *through* you until He does something *to* you! If you choose to build a wall around your heart keeping Him from entering into every part of you, permeating every fiber of your being..., in essence, you have the power to harden your heart even toward almighty Mediator. We're also told if we harden our hearts, we can *not* hear His voice. Consequently, our disobedience is a result of our disbelief. Here, read it for yourself," as this once again rattled Connector handed Elton a copy of the Manual For Life.

Ever since Elton had graduated college prior to the summer, Kindred-Spirit knew he'd have to approach him like a rocket about to blast off into orbit, because Elton *wasn't* a normal Commoner. As a matter of fact, he was as un-normal as one could be at his age.

Elton was in Seeker mode—a Seeker seeking more from life than mediocre. And if it was hard for Kindred-Spirit to tame this young surviving stallion, it was nothing compared to the difficult stirring urges Elton felt. Little did he know just how difficult brokenness would be in the years to come.

"Wow! No disrespect, but I've always been told that passage was referring to Mediator standing on the outside of a lost soul wanting to come into their heart. You don't think it is?" Elton looked intently, hardly willing to believe whatever answer he was about to hear.

"No. I don't. Let me ask you this Elton. Where does it say He is standing on the outside of their heart knocking to get inside their heart?"

"Well, I'm not sure, I guess I just assumed. And heck, that's what I've always been taught. Weren't you?" Elton put on a foul, scowling smirk.

"Of course that's what I was taught back when I was your age. But I came to realize that so many teach passages like these from misconceptions."

"Yeah, but that's what I'm wondering," Elton leaned forward again eagerly. "Where did these misconceptions come from? Who in the world started them? So many things don't make sense to me, especially when I'm beginning to wonder who I can trust anymore."

"Hold on my friend," Kindred-Spirit roared back. "Wisdom would tell you, don't throw the baby out with the bathwater. You need to accept how most Commoners usually pre-suppose something they too have heard all their life. We're all guilty of these presuppositions, finding our niche verses and using them as hinges for everything else. A lot of the time, most never eagerly search to see all the truth with their own eyes." Kindred-Spirit paused to let his words sink in.

Then Elton refocused on the Manual For Life reading the whole passage around that one common verse, "Crazy but I think that might have helped me get it. Isn't this a letter from Mediator to a Local Gathering?... and aren't all Local Gatherings made up of believers in Him?"

"Good insight, Elton. As a matter of fact, look at the final phrase Mediator said, '*He who has an ear, let him hear what the Comforter says to the Local Gatherings*. He's referring to heart ears."

"I'm not sure I understand what it means to hear with my heart ears," Elton humbly admitted.

"Well, according to my favorite Thriver named Paul in the Manual For Life, no one can hear with their mere mind what is written for the human spirit unless they have the Comforter living in their spirit telling them what to believe. Only believers can have the Comforter, right?"

Elton nodded in agreement, "But I'll be honest, at this point in my life, I have a hard time with anyone telling me what to believe."

"Listen my young friend," Kindred-Spirit continued with a straight face plastered beneath what were once stoic eyes, "It's similar to the phrase Mediator used with His followers after miraculously feeding the four thousand, just a few weeks after they complained about the feeding of the five thousand, '*Why do you discuss the fact that you have no bread? Do you **still** not see or understand? Do you have a hardened heart? Having eyes, do you not see? And having ears, do you not hear?*' Elton, may I also add, do you not see or hear according to who you are in your spirit? Who are you really, Elton? Are you a true follower and have you experienced the exchanged life, yet?"

He gazed miserably into the parking lot. More than anything else, Elton wanted to find his niche in life. He wanted freedom to experience the passions locked deep inside his Innermost Being to be a true follower of Mediator. But, due to the performance-based system, he had the hardest time wrapping his mind around these naggings beneath his soul. Plus, competing for his emotions, his intentions were with another relationship. He wanted to find that once-in-a-life-time connection with the girl of his dreams, Elaine—a relationship spanning the course of a lifetime without the fear of getting rejected. He was trying to understand the deeper meaning of his life, but common explanations on the streets of Suburb of Soul just weren't satisfying his inner hunger.

"I'm not sure who I am, Kindred-Spirit. So what are Inner Longings, anyway? And how can I have hope for the solution to become a true follower of Mediator? With all my baggage and identity crisis, what the heck could I ever exchange for eternal life?" he asked in a bit of frustration and discouragement.

"In case you haven't heard, my friend, the source of the Life Exchanger's solution is always bigger than the source of your problem. But, before you can have hope for the solution, you must first have a reason for hope. Listen Elton, you've got to dig deeper beneath the soul in order to understand your Inner Longings. The Life Exchanger gave them to you when you already exchanged your old dead spirit in Adam for your new eternal life in Mediator. In fact, He did this so you'd seek fulfillment for your unique meaning and purpose according to His plan for your life. However, only by being exchanged for life on a daily basis can you acquire becoming a Thriver—something that eludes your preconceived notions as a surviving Commoner taught by the Pselfologists," wise Connector said.

"So my soul, apart from my new identity in Mediator, is mainly about Self wanting to be in control?" Elton tried to keep it simple.

Suddenly Elton sat upright on his booth seat. He had been staring absent-mindedly into the neighboring table, and the table was staring back at him. Elton jumped back startled as an enormous voice floated across the aisle.

"Pretty much. But the soul has other needs too... needs for more than temporal soulish things in a material world."

It was old man Tucker from the green moss-covered rooftop A-frame, down on the lake near the dam. He liked butting in conversations randomly without an invitation.

"Forget about that for right now," hurled Kindred-Spirit. "Mind your business Tucker! I'm talking with the boy. Ok, let's get back on track with your Inner Longings. They come from your Innermost Being and long to be a true follower. Your Inner Longings need hope for your spiritual heart, which compete with Self over your soul. Unfortunately, like Tucker said, many surviving Commoners like you in Suburb of Soul build walls of protection for various other reasons—including a boycott on what the Manual For Life calls *dying-to-Self.*"

"Dying to Self!" Elton contemplated with an uncontrollable outburst. "What in the world does that mean?"

"Oh my young friend, you still have so much to learn. Even Commoners, who call themselves believers, conspicuously live independent of the Life Exchanger's provision for protection from Self destruction—something keeping their fleshly nature unsatisfied and always seeking more soulish pleasures. A trick, I might add, from the enemy, Rejector, who is seeking to devour you by the day in the faulty system. He is subtly killing, stealing, and destroying everyone's hope for freedom. True freedom comes by becoming a follower of Mediator in the Spirit by grace."

"I'm still confused, Kindred-Spirit. Sounds like Commoners are their own worst enemies... not just Rejector."

"Well put my friend... well put." Connector paused with a sigh and a lingering sadness in his eye.

"So is this the way things have always been in Suburb of Soul?... I mean, were all my ancestors the same way from the beginning?" Elton was eager for more answers to his usually unspoken questions.

"No, not always, but this is very difficult to explain. So buckle your seatbelt as I take you through a quick rundown of some rough terrain," Kindred-Spirit replied. "This is the part where you need to pay close attention as I explain more about Self's *flesh*. If you can imagine, there was a time when things turned from bad to worse. In remarkable fashion, Rejector—through Suburb of Soul—began to provide all the convenient amenities of the worldly life indulging Self's *flesh*, while preserving the chivalry, in down-home style, fit for Self's *faith*. According to the Manual For Life, after many attempts, as the architect, Rejector finally figured out how to surmise a plan to counterfeit the contrast of half truths by combining soul and spirit into a fancy word known as dichotomy. Commoners abandoned the original trichotomous truths taught by Mediator's original chosen followers. Over the years, Self-reliant Commoners began targeting their *soulical* needs independent of the Life Exchanger. They began living more and more Self-sufficient lives, despite the Life Exchanger's provisions for *spiritual* life (*ruach* in the Hebrew and *Zoe* in the Greek). Unfortunately, Commoners neglected the teachings of the Manual For Life, by integrating vain philosophies of the Pselfologists with compelling arguments in a modern world based on common human traditions and customs—basically manmade systems. They learned to survive by their soul without thriving with their spirit. Commoners were no longer focused on Mediator with their spiritual eyes and ears. That's how a Commoner's identity resorts to soulish ways in Suburb of Soul believing with their mind all their lives."

"Is it ok for my soul to know my Self, or is that bad? I mean, doesn't my soul need saving?" Elton asked an inquisitive question.

"Great question, Elton. You're on the right track, but consider this. Mediator never told anyone He was seeking to save peoples souls, did He? As a matter of fact, He made it perfectly clear when asking a redundant question, *'what can a man give in exchange for his soul,'* (in the Greek, soul-life). Listen, there is absolutely nothing in this world Commoners can give for their soul-life in exchange for eternal life. Eternal life is spiritual in nature. On the contrary, He came to give everyone a new spirit-life in exchange for their dead spirit. It is only by grace through faith can a person receive what is given by the Spirit. And that my friend, requires a choice to believe with your human spirit—the part of you that was made in His image."

"No one's ever told me this before," Elton pondered for a moment. "Wow! So where in the Manual For Life does it say we are... what did you call it... tri... tripod... tripodomous?"

"Trichotomous, ...silly survivor," Kindred-Spirit chuckled over the young mans delightful innocence. "I'll give you a couple to chew on and maybe you can commit them to memory. First, my favorite is, *'May Life Exchanger Himself, the Exchanger of peace, sanctify you through and through. May your whole spirit, soul, and body be kept blameless at the coming of our Lord, Mediator. The one who calls you is faithful and He will do it.'* And then there's, *'For the Word of Life Exchanger is living and active and sharper than any double edged sword, it penetrates even to dividing soul—"*

"*—and spirit...*" Elton chimed in, *"...joints and marrow; it judges the thoughts and attitudes of the heart.'* Yeah, I memorized that one when I was just a kid. Ummm... so why and when did Commoners change their beliefs?"

"Another fantastic question," Kindred-Spirit affirmed his young apprentice. "You see, they changed their beliefs because Rejector manipulated their minds a long time ago to change their values with persuasive arguments appealing to man-made traditions. You gotta get that. That's the number one evil scheme of all times... MANIPULATION!" Kindred-Spirit practically shouted for everyone to hear. "But for true followers, as citizen saints, not everyone understands how Self can only find *True Identity* by exchanging the old in Adam, for the new in

Mediator. However, as you can imagine, things often get overlooked when strong urges deep within each Commoner's flesh tries to justify selfish choices by doing good deeds of Self-righteousness. Most think that's how they are to win the favor of The Life Exchanger. In fact, recorded in the Manual For Life, the one who got swallowed up by a big fish and burped up on a beach, was clinging to worthless idols forfeiting the grace that *could* be his. The life lesson?... there's a struggle in each believers Self between two natures: the nature of flesh (worldly desires) and the nature of the spirit (righteous desires). In his case, he was battling between two natures: clinging to his worthless idols and forfeiting the grace that could be his. But only one nature is who we really are. You can't be two natures at the same time, can you? Elton, listen, discovery can only happen when the passions of your heart experience an exchanged spirit-life from your old identity in Adam, to your new identity in Mediator. But make no mistake about it, you must die to Self in order to become alive in Him."

"But the performance-based system is all I've ever known," Elton said in a boyish wine. "In fact, all the Commoners here in Suburb of Soul teach only one way to live... nothing about two natures flip flopping back and forth."

"Hmmm... yes my young friend, strikingly different from what's commonly known. However, the performance-based system exists in contrast to freedom through the Grace-based system. Amazing Grace—as it has been called a time or two—can only happen when the Life Exchanger finishes the good work *He* began in each true believer's spirit. Then, and only then, can Mediator live *through* you. Unfortunately, the one thing holding your true identity back from your new nature is the insatiable hunger of the flesh, which ferociously wants control ...and is more than afraid to let go."

"Do you always speak in riddles, old man? You sound more like one of the old prophets who foretold the future in the past. I need you to help me ...but I need it simple. Try to understand, the one thing I struggle with the most, is when I've heard you say over and over again that I have to exchange my *old* man in Adam for my *new* man in Mediator. If I recall correctly, wasn't Mediator impressed by the man who said, '*I know what I do believe… help me in my unbelief!*' Kindred-Spirit, that's me. I think I get the whole flesh versus the spirit thing in my head when I read it in the Manual For Life… but I still don't get the dying to Self thing in my heart in order to have freedom. What do I have to do to get freedom?"

Kindred-Spirit smiled, grinning from ear to ear. "I like you Elton. Your blunt and straightforward approach is refreshing. I've not known many young men quite like you in your generation who know the Manual For Life so well and ask such insightful questions. There's something special about you. However, to answer your question about Self and freedom, you see, in Suburb of Soul, Self is often identified by the labels Pselfologists ascribe. You know… like the generations they're born into. For example, you've heard of the Great Depression that produced the Old Schoolers? And then there are the Baby Boomers and the X-generation. That's why it's nearly impossible for young men like yourself, in your generation, influenced by good-Ole-boy macho men, to overcome these misleading mentalities by a world conditioned to conform and perform. Yet, the vicious cycle is about to come full circle for Commoners like you whose lives eventually spiral out of control. It's usually when an intimate relationship sabotages everything. You young men only think you conquer your damsel in distress. I'm hear to tell you, with a stroke of genius, I have confidence in you Elton that you'll eventually put all the straight edges together, building a framework around the middle in order to showcase the most significant piece to the puzzle. Something you'll need to eventually discover about relationships… the *Fair Exchange!* But you'll probably crash and burn before you do."

"Gee, thanks. Come on, man," Elton squirmed in his chair, "I don't have a clue as to what you're talking about. Why can't you give me simple explanations to my simple questions?"

"Because there's absolutely nothing simple about your questions when you try to reason spiritual truths with your soulish mind, my friend. In fact, most

Commoners won't even attempt to dive *this* deep. Listen, most are plagued by an epidemic to be politically correct, living on the edge of worldly philosophies. Most modern Local Gatherings—like the one you've grown up in—choose to separate their contemporary practices from original teachings found in the Manual For Life. No matter how you look at it right now, if you keep searching, sooner or later Comforter will help you discover the truth as to how Suburb of Soul is desperately trying to maintain order in what some are calling a post-modern culture. And yet, with a glimmer of hope, there's something stirring in the bowels of the land where teachings of old are becoming new again. Exchanged lives are growing in numbers where only transformed believers know the real supernatural difference between Self-centered desires in their mind, versus Mediator-centered living in their spirit. Elton, I hope you're beginning to see with your heart eyes, in order to be a true follower of Him, it's only by the anointing of the Comforter—who is real, not counterfeit!"

"Well, you're right about one thing, old-timer, what I've been taught is very different from what you're teaching. Even our pastor, Brother Delegator, says in his sermons that the Life Exchanger only helps those who help themselves. Heck, just the other Sunday he even said to us young men, if we're lucky, we'll find ourselves a better half and become complete through everlasting bliss here on earth."

Kindred-Spirit, in a sarcastic tone, responded back, "And is that what seems to captivate the essence of a covenant of love between a young groom and his young bride in blessed holy matrimony … two halves complete one another? Come on Elton, only Mediator can complete you …not Elaine."

"Well, that's not what I hear on the streets. Either way, I want to enjoy Elaine, sharing all my Inner Longings with her for the rest of my life."

"Sure. I understand," Kindred-Spirit released a big sigh, expressing a little sympathy in his voice, "unlike the unrealistic expectations taught in Suburb of Soul, you must envision by faith the hopeful anticipation of how you and Elaine will take on the world and conquer your dreams together. Once you've learned how to die to Self and can unconditionally connect your hearts for a lifetime, then and only then, can you know what it means '*Til Death Do Us* **Start**,' before you exchange the vow '*Til Death Do Us* **Part**! You see, the life exchange you need to discover together, isn't usually taught by your parents at home in front of a box, or teachers in scheduled meetings with programs. Be careful not to compare this to the wrong thing."

"Heck, Kindred-Spirit, I don't know anything to compare this to. Your ideas are off the chart!"

"Well, hopefully you'll see sooner or later. In any case, it's been my experience that life from its conception for most Commoners has been filled with oxymorons and paradoxes in a labyrinth full of contradictions. You only think you were raised from a pretty normal—maybe even typical—mentality among Commoners. But the Manual For Life was not intended for your mind. It can only be discerned by a believer's spirit. Not in keeping with Suburb of Soul, if your desire is to become a true follower of Mediator, it requires a journey to the HeartLand."

"But what about living in Suburb of Soul? It's normal for my soul to be full of thoughts and emotions with spiritual ideas, right?"

"That's what we were all taught, my young friend. In fact, if you consider what I'm saying by searching for answers in the Manual For Life, without any real apparent reason or explanation for your mind, those ideas will seem pretty foolish. Of course, what's natural and obvious are the external five senses your body craves in relationships. Those, I'm sure you can easily relate to when seeking happiness from loneliness for your Self." Kindred-Spirit leaned his head back looking up at the ceiling then back at the blank stare in Elton's eyes. "I know. I know. Too many big words and concepts again. But bear with me, son, all these details are leading up to something absolutely amazing you'll discover about the Great Exchange.

But you must experience Mediator living *through* you!—and I promise *not* to lecture much more."

They both laughed and took a break to eat their sub sandwiches.

~

While walking out of the restaurant, Kindred-Spirit said, "Ok Elton, likewise to all that stuff about being a true follower of Mediator, let me warn you about one last thing. It has to do with your relationship with Elaine. You need to realize how confusing it can be distinguishing between how we are all human being made in the image of our creator, yet there are the parts of us unlike each other in our gender differences. Internally, you've probably tried to wrap your mind around why you've been taught that guys are predominately Logical-Thinkers, while girls are primarily Emotional-Feelers, right? Well, if you recall, externally, you've been told guys are masculine for their muscles, while girls are feminine for their figures. Heck, you've probably even considered the vain philosophy that men are from Mars and women are from Venus, yet somehow made in the image of their Creator to cohabitate earth together."

"Yep," Elton replied with a smirk. But even for him, after while, this sounded way too mechanical for his beliefs on what makes up the differences between males and females.

Kindred-Spirit continued, "…well, rather than turning to popular explanations from the Pselfologists, always table your questions toward the Manual For Life. It declares men and women are *equal* partners in the grace of life. Just make sure you're on the same page about who you follow before making any big decisions. Walk in grace, my friend, and I'll call you later."

That's all the stimulation Elton needed for inspiration regarding his *intentions* toward Elaine.

Chapter 1 Journey Journal

Like Elton, we can all relate as Commoners in Suburb of Soul at one time or another. More than likely, we've all heard the Great Commission: *"Go therefore and make **disciples**."* (Matt. 28:18 & 19).

What do you believe is the biblical (Manual For Life) meaning of the word discipleship for you personally?

_____

_____

_____

_____

When the Bible (Manual For Life) uses the term discipleship (follower), it is referring to someone who has completely surrendered to Jesus (Mediator) and is faithfully—not perfectly—living a life devoted to Him from the Inside-out perspective. It literally implies that a believer is to be a "learner" who has ears to hear and eyes to see. And yet, each one must put down any kind of wall of protection around their heart. Whenever you are tempted to blame others for your problems, look at what Jesus said to His disciples in Mark 8 verses 16-17: *"They (the disciples) discussed (complained or blamed each other) this with one another and said, 'It is because we have no bread.' Aware of their discussion, Jesus asked them: 'Why are you talking about having no bread? Do you <u>still</u> not see or understand? Are your hearts hardened?'"*

How can you relate to the disciples complaining/blaming and hardening their hearts when things don't work out in your life?

_____

_____

_____

_____

In contrast to complaining with a bad attitude, Kindred-Spirit encouraged Elton to look at what a believer exchanges in return—a healthy attitude. Thus, a disciple should exhibit a faithful, teachable, approachable, and available heart with a grateful attitude characterizing integrity. In fact, the word disciple in the Greek (didaskalos) is found in the Bible only in the Gospels and the book of Acts. It is a name given to the follower or scholar or pupil of any teacher, and is someone who believes and helps spread the doctrine (teaching) of another among the community (Suburb of Soul). In all cases it implies that the person not only accepts the views of the teacher (Connector), but adheres to and practices their teachings. As in Matt. 9:14, it is sometimes applied to the followers of John the Baptist, and even of the Pharisees in 22:16. But principally to the followers of Christ, Matt. 10:24; Luke 10:1; 14:26, 27, 33; John 6:69; Acts 9:26; 14:20; 21:4. The first time disciples were ever called Christians was at Antioch, Acts 11:26.

Therefore, a disciple of Christ after the resurrection is one who: (1) believes His doctrine (teaching), (2) rests on His sacrifice, (3) is filled with the indwelling of His Spirit, and (4) imitates his example.

Like Paul the apostle was to young Timothy, so Kindred-Spirit was a mentoring Connector to Elton. Why is it so important for every believer to be discipled in the Exchanged For Life principles?

_____

_____

_____

_____

Notice how Jesus (Mediator) modeled a Master-learner relationship with His followers on a personal level. The four Gospels in the New Testament clearly show that the word "disciple" can refer to others besides the original 12. The verb "follow" became something of a personal term Jesus used to call His disciples, who were then called followers (Mark 4:10). These "followers" included a larger company of people from whom He selected the twelve (Mark 3:7-19; Luke 6:13-17). This larger group included both men and women (Luke 8:1-3; 23:49) from all walks of life like: fisherman, accountants, a doctor, and yes… even tax collectors, zealots, and prostitutes. Jesus was no doubt popular among the social outcasts and religiously despised, but people of wealth and theological prestige also followed (Luke 8:1-3; 19:1-10; John 3:1-3; 12:42; 19:38-39).

All "followers" of Jesus, after the personal account in the four gospels of Jesus' journey with His disciples, the book of Acts frequently uses the term "disciple" to refer generally to all the followers who believe in the risen Lord (6:1-2,7; 9:1,10,19,26,38; 11:26,29).

What then does it really mean to be a follower of Jesus as our Mediator between us and God (The Life Exchanger)?

_____

_____

_____

_____

To begin to understand our call to discipleship, we would do well to start where Jesus called his first disciples. Scripture (Manual For Life) gives us some interesting insights into the lives of these men and women. As we look more closely, we will begin to understand more about what it truly means to call ourselves a follower of Christ. However, just as these divinely inspired truths revealed by God's Spirit (Comforter) set forth in the response of these men, we too need to recognize and acknowledge Christ's call by His Spirit in our spiritual heart rather than the mental and emotional response of our soul.

Jesus' call to His first disciples was simply "follow me," "come after me," "learn from me." Further study shows that the Greek word translated "follow" means to accompany or to be in the same way with. It's the same word which describes a flock of sheep going along behind their shepherd. The call here for people is simple: "Follow me with your heart."

What do you imagine motivated the first believers (Commoners)—from the little we know about each individual—to give up their "soul-life" as they knew it, to follow this divine Mediator, Jesus? And, how could they possibly entertain the idea of leaving behind all that they knew (in Suburb of Soul) to step out into the unknown?

_____

_____

_____

_____

Like Elton, how do you think or feel the disciple's families and friends reacted to their sudden decision?

_____

_____

_____

_____

Like Elton contemplating his future journey away from Suburb of Soul, what do you believe the disciples were expecting life to be like as they followed Jesus away from the life they'd always known (man-made faulty systems)?

_____

_____

_____

_____

Most of us come from a "what's in it for me" mentality like Elton. Whenever someone asks us to do something, we are programmed from a performance-based society to question how it will benefit our "Self." Jesus said in Luke 9:23, *"If anyone wishes to come after me, let him deny himself* (soul-life in the flesh), *and take up his cross daily, and follow me."*

What do you believe Jesus meant when telling His disciples to deny their "Self" daily?

_____

_____

_____

_____

Elton was not only intrigued by Kindred-Spirit's knowledge, he was very eager to get answers to some itching questions. In the book of Acts we read about the Berean Jews who were eager to learn: *"Now these* (Berean Jews) *were more noble-minded than those* (Jews) *in Thessalonica, for they received the word with great eagerness, examining the Scriptures daily to see whether these things were so."* (Acts17:11).

Describe your level of eagerness to learn the Exchanged For Life principles as a follower of Jesus (Mediator).

_____

_____

_____

_____

Even though Jesus oftentimes determines extreme levels of personal sacrifices (including forsaking loved ones, losing health–property–possessions-finances-careers-accomplishments and even social status, etc. Matt. 4:18-22; 10:24-42; Luke 5:27-28; 9:57-62; 14:25-27; 18:28-30), the commitment of "discipleship" might actually scare you.

What do you struggle with the most when challenged to be a sold out follower of Jesus?

_____

_____

_____

_____

Chapter 2

Waking up to a Big Dream

A s time passed, Elton continued working hard climbing the ladder at his good paying job. All the while he held tightly to his precious china-cup, Elaine. Mysteriously, something about a Big Dream—with all its empowering grace—eluded our young Commoner. Not a simpleton by any stretch of the imagination, Elton struggled with the idea of how Mediator seeks to live *through* believers. This Logical Thinker, unbeknownst to the better part of his judgment, was about to encounter his own Big Dream.

In fine fashion with faithful satisfaction, he was a committed believer, who was obligated to those in leadership at the Local Gathering. He enjoyed the benefit of community with his friends and family, so he showed respect to the elders. Although some of the them were formally-trained in expository style, others followed denominational traditions. One former Evangelist in particular, Brother Delegator, left his travels to lead his crusade near the mountains. He taught straight from the so-called inspired translation of the Manual For Life, holding tightly to the performance-based gospel for the soul. He believed the way to touch the heart was through thoughts and emotions.

Due to the masterful surmise of the Governor of Suburb of Soul named Dictator—the brother of Brother Delegator—Commoners were prohibited from entertaining the ridiculous idea of venturing outside the boundaries of Suburb of Soul, especially to pursue a Big Dream. As a matter of fact, if any Commoner accepted an invitation, they would certainly be ostracized with all kinds of fear, shame, guilt and pain, which led to the ultimate consequence …rejection!

On the other hand, especially for Elton, the alternative was not too inviting either. Accepting an invitation meant facing a conflict with his family, encounter brokenness, surrender Self-control, and forfeit all the provisions from his comfort zone's point of view back at his nicely modified Perspective Home.

Yet, the conflicting nagging urge to fulfill the Big Dream already had a certain appeal deep within his Inner Longings. Strangely, he admired from a distance some folks, Ponder and Sympathy, at the Local Gathering who accepted the challenge and were about to take a big risk. They too lived life from a more simple perspective at first. Ponder was the Music Director for a few years. Then their nagging urges grew stronger and stronger until an invitation in the middle of the night rocked them in their sleep. They accepted the challenge and announced their resignation. Needless to say, their status changed dramatically at the Local Gathering and on the streets of Suburb of Soul.

Now, one Sunday morning after service, they recognized that look in Elton's eyes. So they invited him to their Perspective Home for lunch, hoping to help him mull things over along with Elaine.

"I have noticed something about you two since you quit leading music," Elton engaged in conversation over lunch. "You're not the same …in a good way, I mean. You seem different now, unlike all the other Commoners at the Local Gathering."

"Yeah… how so?" Ponder asked in a calm demeanor.

"I mean, don't get me wrong, but I've noticed you have a kind of joy and peace on your face unlike your normal stoic smiles you wore to worship."

Sympathy chuckled in a friendly laugh, "That's sweet of you to notice, Elton." She leaned back covering her mouth with her napkin. "I'm not laughing at you, I've just intuitively known there's something different about you, too."

"So how's your family?" Awkwardly, Elton tried to change the subject, not wanting the attention on himself.

Ponder, recognizing the avoidance, redirected this ship back on course. "Oh, my parents are great! Sympathy's parents along with mine are planning a big trip with us. Funny thing, we all experienced the same Big Dream that rocked us in our sleep. We're all leaving soon for the HeartLand in the Misty Mountains. In fact, our Connector was in town not long ago and invited us all to travel with him."

"You mean... you're going to.... I mean, you and your parents are...," Elton just couldn't get the words out.

"Yes, Elton, we're all taking a risk and going to the HeartLand in the Misty Mountains to pursue our Big Dream. You see, after my mishap with my flesh patterns getting in the way of leading music, I devastated my whole family. Sympathy and I hit rock bottom in our relationship and I just about lost everything. Oddly enough, though, just when things looked their worse, we were all visited the same night and given an invitation to pursue our Big Dream."

"Yeah but... that's all behind you now. You seem so happy to me living here from your Perspective Home and joyful at the Local Gathering. What do you mean you're seeking your Big Dream?" Elton shuttered at the thought of his friends leaving Suburb of Soul.

"Elton," Ponder said gently, "try to look at it this way; if anyone ever takes a risk to pursue their Big Dream, it means they pursue a quest—our quest is just a stone's throw away from the HeartLand in the majestic Misty Mountains."

Elton was eager to know more, but his body and mind quivered at the possibilities of *rejection*.

"Listen, milk without meat leads to mediocre believers, and we've been so unhappy settling for stale manna without fresh new insights to the abundant life." Sympathy continued to explain, "All connected heart-mates have a growing urge that happens in their relationship sooner or later. Passions either grow so strong you can't control them, or they die out and you can hardly stand your partner anymore. These nagging urges either pursue the very same Inner Longings for something extraordinary just beyond the realm of ordinary, or they become stagnant if you keep them to your Self secretive from each other—including friends and family—and they eventually fade away. But if you embrace your nagging urges, that's when the strange encounter happens."

"What... what strange encounter happens?" Elaine spoke up.

"Well, before we get to the strange encounter, you both need to understand a few things from a common Commoners *perspective*," Ponder said. "You see, settled within the community, tucked away just north of the peaks and valleys of the HeartLand, most Commoners live in the comfort zones of their Perspective Homes nestled among the fortunes of few. This has been the norm for every Commoner ever since the beginning of Suburb of Soul—."

"—Whoa," Elton interrupted, "I know the Connector you've been talking to... Kindred-Spirit!"

"How'd you know?" Elaine turned to Elton and asked. "Did he explain all of this to you already?"

"Kinda. But I want them to keep going. I'd like for us to hear more of their version," as he glanced over at Elaine squeezing her hand tightly.

Ponder continued, "Well, as you probably already know this, but everyone looks at life from their own Perspective Home's vantage point, right? That's where everyone's perception molds their reality. Of course, we were all told to withhold our affections from unwelcomed intruders—like those Seekers." Ponder and Sympathy laughed sarcastically. "As a matter of fact, this came naturally for good-Ole-boy/Old Schoolers like us, even though we were always acting cordially nice on the outside."

"So… you weren't being real?" Elton confronted in confusion.

"No, no. To us, that was being real." Sympathy jumped in. "However, our nagging urges were secretively challenged in one particular way: deep down inside our Innermost Being, we wanted to get off the performance-based treadmill. Unfortunately, it has always been the commonly accepted works-based system of the Human Doers."

"The Human Doers?" Elton questioned.

"That's right, the Human Doers," Sympathy continued, "…they are the ones who are the forgetful hearers, and therefore ineffectual doers. There's a difference you know. Remember, the Manual For Life speaks of the law of liberty when we are to be doers and not just hearers, in spite of our tendency to get sucked into the illusion of control of the human soul. But the Doers I'm talking about are the ones assigned to teach everyone how to manipulate their heart by learning wall-building skills. However, there are Commoners like us who've had an unrelenting urge to find more meaning and purpose in life beyond the common mindset. And now, we're taking the risk to put down our walls of protection. Vulnerable, I know, but we're setting out on an adventure to the HeartLand… even if it means traveling through the Forbidden Forest."

"Be aware of one more thing in the lives of Commoners," Ponder added. "Logical Thinkers tend to think inside the box, Emotional Feelers feel more comfortable within the accepted norm. Even though Logical Thinkers think more objectively, Emotional Feelers, of course, feel more subjectively. But they both have one thing in common, every Commoner has a heart made in the image of their Creator needing Mediator to reconcile between the Life Exchanger and humans, which can only happen by the Comforter's invitation."

"But why?" Elaine was growing weary and disillusioned.

Sympathy tried to reach out with a comforting explanation, "Well Elaine, I know it's hard to take it all in, but let me try and explain it this way. Unfortunately, like two ships passing in the middle of the night, it's always been hard for Logical Thinkers to communicate with fickle Feelers like us, whose emotions are constantly changing our minds. But because we are *sensitive* Feelers, it's hard to communicate with hard-headed Thinkers like Ponder and Elton who think they know it all. So, because of selfish reasons, and without a working knowledge of how to think and feel with our hearts, neither of us can quite see things from each other's Home Perspective. This takes us out of our comfort zones due to the walls of protection guarding our Self-preservation. Consequently, on the more complex level, independent notions usually occupy our selfish motivation because of these hardened *walls* around our hearts—something the Pselfologists completely dismissed as nonsense... but now I know it's true because I've experienced the truth."

"If what you're saying is true, then I feel lied to my entire life. I'm not sure what's real anymore. Who in the world can I trust?" Elaine was struggling and having a bit of a meltdown.

"In case you've ever wondered," Ponder jumped in, "in the course of our weekly routines, everyday choices for taking action were made pretty much the same, right? Woken by clocks, nature sounds, and ringtones, in the morning we get up, take a shower, eat breakfast, and off to work or school we go. When the nine-to-five day-to-day operations, social luncheons, and business meetings are done, we each return to the *comfort zone* of our nice Perspective Homes for the weekend, with one day set aside to worship at Local Gathering. All our daily disciplines are in order. For most dinner decisions, Logical Thinkers like me and Elton usually eat what we think tastes good; you Emotional Feelers eat whatever fits your mood; always eating something from Soul-Food markets and restaurants while constantly keeping on the go. Despite the fading tradition of eating at least one meal a day with family members, most of us lost the notion to ask the other what he or she would like for fear of an argument breaking out. Plus, apart from our values and beliefs, communication has been hard work, especially for us baby-boomers taught by Old-Schoolers leaving the X-generation without a clue, and now a lost generation like yours." They all took a deep breath as this all seemed very sobering when putting it in perspective.

But Elton and Elaine were in a bit of a quandary as the evening came to a close. For some strange, unwelcoming reason, they both knew their lives were about to change drastically if they continued to entertain these *crazy notions*.

~

More time passed.

Elton, if he wasn't hanging with some friends, on the Internet, piddling with some gadget, or busy with some kind of project, would settle into one of his regular adventure shows on the box in his living room. Elaine, if she wasn't reading a novel, shopping with a friend, talking on the phone with her mom, or grooming her nails, liked cozying up to a chick-flick on the big screen box in her family room. Of course, if these single Commoners weren't busy together with sports activities, concert events, or social gatherings, they would watch music videos and entertainment shows on a flat-screen box during their workouts at the local gym or cuddled up in each others arms on the couch.

One day, Elton had a certain thought, Elaine had a certain feeling, which led to certain actions, all of which made them both very uncomfortable about something *big* missing from their lives.

~

Then, as if time stood still, more than a mere coincidence, something very significant and extraordinary happened to each of them at the same time at their separate Perspective Homes late one particular night. Elton and Elaine both woke from a dream that rocked them in their sleep. Compelled by something more than the human will, these were the words swimming among certain thoughts with certain emotions compelling certain actions:

A shroud of clouds hide dusk's beauty, while hope slips quietly into the night. But rising from dawn's visual feast, a promise comes with new light. You already know what you want to do, but you don't know how to do what you know. Soon you'll leave the comfort of your home, when the time comes, you must go. Your answer lies beyond the hills, in a land you cannot see. Find the one you already know, a Connector he will be.

"Could it be?" They each said to their Self. They scurried around in their minds looking for an explanation. Suddenly, it occurred to both of them, the nagging urge was actually coming from their Inner Longings for more meaning and purpose. They'd been told a time or two to be careful of those urges. Unexpectedly however, their uncontrollable urge was not coming from catalogued thoughts or an inventory of emotions they could so easily order from their soul. Instead, these were unfamiliar urges yearning with desires for something that could only be enabled by the Comforter. They later learned that whenever Commoners becoming Seekers, they were destined for a journey to the HeartLand.

From their Perspective Homes, there were showers to be taken and breakfast to be eaten. So they each jumped out of bed to get ready for something new and exciting. Only... Elton and Elaine each discovered something else—a brightly colored package placed on tables resting at the foot of their beds. To their recollections, those weren't there before.

Where did they come from? What do they mean? A quiver of excitement shook their bodies from head to toe as they eagerly opened the packages wrapped around three books inside. With big bold letters on each cover, the top one read Exchanged For Life, the next, Journey Journal, and the one on the bottom was their very own personalized copy of the Manual For Life. Still wrapped in plastic, on the inside pocket of their Journey Journal was a Swiss Army knife-pen with all kinds of bells-n-whistles. Without a shadow of doubt, both concluded they'd been visited by Mediator in a Big Dream.

Now gossip traveled fast when anyone got wind of Commoners encountering Mediator in a Big Dream. Many of those who integrated Pselfologists philosophies were called Flesh-Modifiers, and those who held on dogmatically to rules and regulations called Law-Conformers, passed around rumors according to opinions shared in the community gossip grapevines. Elton and Elaine, it so happened, had heard a time or two some of the nastiest disturbing rumors when Commoners in Suburb of Soul woke up to a Big Dream. But all the propaganda they'd been warned was not anything like their experience! Their Big Dream was confirmed by the gentle voice of Mediator, with a peace for their ears to hear what was only for them to discern with their spirit.

Shockingly, never in a million years did either one think something so spectacular would happen to them. From that day forward, they had something considered rare and immeasurable. And, to most governed by their soul, these gifts were not considered priceless like a rare rookie baseball card; not more valuable than stored up treasures in marble-pillared vaults. It could only be appreciated by those who understood its *true* value by the compelling nature of their Innermost Being.

But who would tell them of the true meaning in order to confirm they'd been visited by Mediator?

For both Elton and Elaine, one thing was sure, they realized they did not receive a Big Dream that was quantifiable in the tangible realm—not qualifiable with empirical flavor from book-knowledge or street wise. Nor did they receive something to be grasped within the vain philosophies of the Pselfologists methods …at least, not by any man-made conventional means. No, these Inner Longings seemed to exist elusively in a spiritual dimension. It was like one of those 3-D magic-eye pictures. You know, where a picture within a picture hides something more important beyond the two-dimensional perspective.

Nevertheless, simply put, they now possessed a deeper understanding, unlike anything they could remember being taught before.

~

Without any time left for a shower or breakfast, they quickly threw on some casual clothes. Their Inner Longings now empowered a new kind of connection, like a driving force from an inner source, permeating every fiber of their being. Both could hardly wait to get to worship and share with good friends and Elders what happened!

But while on their way to Local Gathering, confusing thoughts, fearful emotions, and random expressions began to slow them down. Worried and troubled that their Inner Longings were too special for simple Commoners like them, huge Self-doubt came pouring over them in buckets full of fear, shame, guilt, and pain. What if all the other Commoners would reject them? What if they would make fun of them and not believe them? All the guilt and shame inflicted by Flesh-Modifiers and Law-Conformers would most certainly deny who they are—faithful, true, and righteous—leaving them in a pool of rejection!

Even so, Elton and Elaine were too happy to allow any of those bullies to squelch their enthusiasm. As soon as they had their first break from worship, they met in the fellowship hall where the youth were selling coffee and juice along with cookies and doughnuts to raise support for the next mission trip. Because they couldn't share their dream with anyone else, in unison, as their eyes met, they uncontrollably simultaneously blurted out the news: "I had a Big Dream! Mediator visited me last night and left a package!"

Elton and Elaine paused in ecstatic surprise catching their breath, each with a puzzled look on their face, but neither laughed at the other or judged with contempt. From a burst of joy, they embraced each other, hugging and jumping hysterically up and down like little children.

And then, noticing all the other Commoners staring at them wondering what was all the commotion, they knew…, "Maybe we should keep this to ourselves and share more over lunch," said Elton. "Yeah, your right," said Elaine in total agreement.

As actions speak louder than words, they just nodded their heads and went back to regular fellowship activities.

~

Day after day, week after week, month after month, Elton and Elaine showed up at their normal jobs, relaxing on the weekend to play and enjoyed Sunday more than ever worshipping Mediator at Local Gathering. For the other five workdays, Elton was a Civil engineer, Elaine supervised marketing and sales. Plus they both had other responsibilities as controllers over the shipping and delivery department. But while they worked, their Inner Longings for more meaning and purpose were growing stronger and stronger. Unlike their usual flirtatious interactions, they infectiously sent texts and e-mails back and forth sharing about how wonderful it would be to put off this mundane routine in exchange for their Big Dream. Plus, so many of their wonderful thoughts and feelings growing toward each other were finally expressed at a deeper level — a heart connection.

As their excitement grew even more intense with each passing day, Elton entertained convictions more than mere thoughts and Elaine swelled with intuition more then mere emotions. Both of them were busting at the seams until finally Elton realized he had to tell his significant other that he'd had enough. He'd never be happy unless he pursued his Inner Longings ultimate destiny. Without knowing it, Elaine felt the same way before he even spoke the words. But her confusion was about why Mediator hadn't yet made it possible for her to know what to *do* next. Not recalling any helpful principles from their personal copy of the Manual For Life or readings from any of the sessions in Exchanged For Life, their impulsive choices produced irrational actions and they simply put their tools down and said, "Let's go, we're out of here!"

"Hold on, hold on, now" said Elton. "This is a little *too* irrational and impetuous even for me. I think we have to come up with a plan and strategize what to *do*, first."

"I feel stuck and confused" Elaine puckered a pout from her pretty lips. "None of my emotional feelings feel right about any good solutions. I guess we just need to wait some more."

"What are we waiting for?" declared Elton. "What are we supposed to be *doing* while we wait?"

They grew more and more miserable, desperate for anything to make them feel better.

More time passed as the Frustration mounted with Resentment, which increased into Anger that led to Bitterness, which they unfortunately took out on each other. As if looking in a mirror, the pressure was building like a volcano about to erupt in each of them. They both felt sick as if there was something churning inside about to B-A-R-F its way out of their flesh!

"This isn't what we were made to *do*," they'd keep reminding each other.

After a while, Self-doubt began to take its toll on their souls. They started to question maybe this was all a big hoax. Someone was having a big laugh at their expense. Rejection was setting in and taking its toll. They felt isolated and alone due to the sense of disapproval and abandonment from other Commoners around them. Consequently, they were losing hope and growing Desensitized, Demotivated, and Defeated by the day.

And then, something was about to happen neither were prepared for.

Chapter 2 Journey Journal

Our journey is a quest. Interestingly, the English word "quest" according to Webster's Dictionary means: a search or pursuit made in order to find or obtain something. The best way to find any answer is to ask the right *questions*. Consider your answer carefully to this next question:

Like Elton and Elaine, have you had a situation in your life that made you stop and wonder, contemplate, and even consider the idea you might have a Big Dream?   Yes or No   If yes, what do you believe is your Big Dream?

_____

_____

_____

_____

Unfortunately, controlling people can squelch our Big Dreams, dominating by means of manipulation, achieving their own Self-serving agendas. We read in the Bible (Manual For Life) that God (the Life Exchanger) gives grace to the humble. And yet, bad leadership does not go unnoticed or unpunished. Often times in the community where we fellowship and worship (the Local Gathering), a leader (Brother Delegator and Dictator) in powerful positions can become master-manipulators more than most would like to admit. As long as other believers (Commoners) around us accept their tyrannizing ways as normal, we tend to feel obligated to follow along; that is, if we want to be accepted. I would only ask that you consider these words from the heart of Mediator, Christ Jesus, in the Scripture for all those shepherds in leadership positions and those sheep under their authority to hear: "*Everyone who is proud in heart is an abomination to the Lord; assuredly he will not be unpunished... For it is time for judgment to begin with the family of God; and if it begins with us, what will the outcome be for those who do not obey the gospel of God?... Test yourselves to see if you are in the faith... Discipline those who continue to sin, rebuke in front of the rest of the church...What business is it of mine to judge those outside the church? Are you not to judge those inside? God will judge those outside. Expel the wicked man from among you... An overseer [elder, shepherd, leader/caregiver] must hold fast the faithful word [the word that is full of faith] which is in accordance with the teachings, that he may be able both to exhort in sound doctrine and to refute those who contradict. For there are many rebellious men, empty talkers and deceivers, especially those of the circumcision (legalism), who must be silenced because they are upsetting whole families... having a form of godliness but denying it's power. Have nothing to do with them!" Proverbs 16:5; I Peter 4:17; II Corinthians 13:5; I Timothy 5:22; I Corinthians 5:12 & 13; Titus 1:9 & 10; II Timothy 3:5.*

Have you ever felt pressure to conform and perform to a leader or leadership that manipulates and controls with fear-based tactics? Yes or No If yes, explain in what way you felt fear's paralyzing power over you.

_____

_____

_____

_____

No matter how difficult our circumstances, we cannot blame others for neglecting our own needs in the choices we make (including when we choose not to choose, we're still the one who made a choice on our own behalf). Therefore, have you neglected your Big Dream because you're too afraid of other people (Flesh-modifiers and Law-Conformers) rejecting you? Yes or No If yes, describe how you might feel like it's all your fault.

_____

_____

_____

_____

Researchers say that about 95% of our reality depends on our perspective (Perspective Home). We all are inclined to rely on what we perceive from our circumstances when we make choices. From your vantage point, describe your perspective of others expectation of you who are most important and influential in your life.

_____

_____

_____

_____

Because the wall of protection consists of fear, shame, guilt, and pain, which leads to rejection, most people try to avoid intimacy in relationships that do not feel safe. Therefore, you may feel that vulnerability is disillusioning and unsafe because people tend to take advantage and use your personal information against you later. Sadly, like the prophet Jonah who got burped up on a beach, we too will even forfeit the grace of God by holding on to our worthless idols (crazy notions) giving us a false sense of security (comfort zone).

What idols are your weak-willed areas in your flesh (comfort zone) that you've become dependant on to keep you from feeling vulnerable to all the fear, shame, guilt, and pain that typically keeps you avoiding rejection?

_____

_____

_____

_____

The worse part of being a victim to controlling master-manipulators is when it causes us to loose confidence in our Big Dream and especially doubting who we are. We find ourselves ultimately doubting our identity because we begin to believe something is wrong with "me."

If you've gradually lost confidence in your Big Dream and especially in who you are, describe what you believe is the one major thing you struggle with the most as a survivor.

_____

_____

_____

_____

Chapter 3

Identity, "Who Am I?"

O ne Friday evening after a week full of overtime, Elton decided to spend some well overdue alone time with Elaine at his Perspective Home. He was hoping to share a nice dinner and a movie… so he told her. Nearly planned for over a month, he finally settled his struggle with commitment in his mind—despite the unknowing underneath his wall-protected heart. He was finally willing to pursue a lifelong covenant if he got the right vibe from his potential future bride. Plus, out of recent shame and guilt heaped on him by his mother, Enabler, a disturbing incident provoked the pride of his damaged ego to finally pop the big question.

As the sun's rays were slowly dipping into a pillow of ruby colored clouds, streaks of lightning pierced the dark shadows just above the horizon. The two of them would soon be retreating into the sunroom dining inside for two, as the rain spoiled the patio ambiance. Knowing her not-so-romantic-boyfriend's struggle with meal plans, Elaine rode separate in her yellow Mustang stopping by for some Soul Food. Elton zoomed home in his compact Spitfire with four on the floor, arriving at his Perspective Home in speedy fashion on the back roads.

Like a dress rehearsal, Elton talked to his Self out loud. He asked Self what he thought would be a romantic food to eat. He then chuckled as he considered what Elaine would probably say, "I'm fine with whatever fits the mood." Like so many times before, they'd both more than likely sit in silent awkwardness, making no decision at all. Aggravated at the thought of it, this spoiled any attempt at a romantic mood for the kind of surprise he had in mind. So he pondered about some solutions. Then he pondered some more. As he pondered, his mind wondered. Nothing was clicking to help his hopeless state of confusion.

Distracted by his frustration, still pondering about how things were soon to play out, Elton was usually the one who'd express his thoughts initially, while Elaine would usually hesitate internalizing how she felt. Followed by superficial gestures, they'd glance at each other wearing those appeasing looks on their faces, both reluctant to share their thoughts and feelings as infatuations kept them both from spoiling their happiness. Humbly, Elton had to be prepared for the worse case scenario, just in case Elaine sent him mixed messages. He'd become a master at avoiding rejection along with other uncomfortable conflicts, so he knew quite well how he'd shift the subject if he wasn't feeling the vibes.

"Well..." as he continued the conversation with his Self, "Elaine would probably hesitate in her pouty way, then finally spill her guts in that sweet innocent whiny voice of hers, ...I'm actually very sad. In fact, I'm growing sadder and sadder every day that I can't pursue my Inner Longings. This whole thing is starting to really upset me... a lot!"

"Yeah," Elton interrupted his Self with an Eeyore tone to his voice, "I think I'm starting to become discontent with my regular job. In fact, the more I ponder these discouraging thoughts, the more I realize how illogical all this really is. Maybe we've made a big mistake—"

Just about then, Elton heard a voice chime in from the garage,

"—For sure," Elaine confirmed. "I'm about as bored as I can be doing the same old routine one, two, three. Each and every day goes by without someone to share my every Inner Longing. Just meaningless busy work, day in and day out.

What's the purpose? I just want to quit my meaningless job and get on with my Big Dream!"

"Hey, Elaine," Elton was surprised at her presence. "How long were you standing there listening to me talk to my Self?"

"Oh, you know, long enough to figure out how these conversations typically go. I'm sure I didn't miss anything, right?"

They both laughed as the mood returned light and pleasant, capturing the flirtatious flavor of two lovebirds getting giddy over nothing.

"Sorry, but I haven't been able to figure out what I think I want for dinner, yet." Elton apologized.

"Well," Elaine replied, not knowing Elton was thinking something more special than normal, "I stopped by and grabbed some good stuff at Soul-FoodMart on my way here. There's plenty of your favorite pasta along with chicken-n-dumplings or we can grill burgers with some fries… I hope that's Ok?"

"Ok? …oh, that's perfect!" Elton exclaimed with a feeling of relief.

So they eventually sat by the glowing fire showcased in the mouth of stone teeth underneath a woodcarved mantle in the living room. Both shared effortlessly more unbelievable details surpassing thoughts and feelings, while dining in the delight of each others company—a visual feast to say the least. Mutually, they decided to leave the big screen off. Before they knew it, hours had passed while contemplating their Big Dreams, getting excited in vigorous conversation all over again. They reminisced about what happened that particular magical night when Mediator visited each of them in a dream and rocked them in their sleep.

Then, as Elaine eloquently described her new inner sentiments, it triggered Elton's memory of something he'd thought for a long, long time. In fact, his was not nearly as new as he'd thought in recent days. As a risk-taking Commoner since early childhood, he'd had these Inner Longings stirring in him before. Something was different on a hot summer night in '69 during a camp retreat. The more the youth leader talked about who the Mediator intended for all Commoners to become in their heart, Elton realized who he became at the moment of his salvation.

Only, at this very moment, he was choosing to connect his Inner Longings need for more meaning and purpose with the doe of his youth for the rest of his life. Elton was still under the impression that connecting with his better half will make him a more complete person. His identity was wrapped up in his status from a single man to a married husband — co-dependency in the making for sure.

Settled in each others arms sipping from the same cup, minutes close to an hour passed. Elaine's eyes began to fill with tears, "My need for Identity is not just a feeling anymore, is it?" She blurted out, "After reading Exchanged For Life, I've experienced a *knowing* deep inside my heart about who I was always born to be — a Seeker and a Thriver! True Identity is all about knowing who I am in the one you introduced me to — Mediator. He wants to live *through* me. I realize now what the Manual For Life says about dying to my soulish Self-centered life, in order to be alive spiritually! Wow, no one ever told me about this stuff my whole life until now."

"So what's the matter, Elaine?" Elton asked with a sympathetic concern. "You sound like something's bothering you in a new way, rather than being happy. Have you changed your beliefs and values about the Exchanged Life?"

"Yes, as a matter of fact I have!" Elaine announced. "I'm finally getting it. I believe an Exchanged Life means exchanging who we were trying to become — "

" — Yeah, in order to become who we were always meant to be... and to be *with*!" Elton finished her sentence ...and a little bit more. He couldn't believe those last four words slipped from his lips expressing his intentions so effortlessly. And so with that perfect segue, Elton popped the question, and Elaine did not disappoint this young warrior's conquest.

With a surge of emotions, Elaine grabbed Elton's face and landed a juicy one on his lips. They relished the thoughts together embracing each other with explosive feelings. Talking was no longer an option in this moment of emotionally charged passion. Sensing a deeper connection than ever before, they got lost in a moment of ecstasy not knowing it could quickly fulfill an immoral fantasy… soulish desires craving Fleshly seduction if they weren't careful.

Interrupting the mesmerizing moment in front of the cozy fire, suddenly the phone rang. Elaine sprang like a bug from her lounging position into Elton's shoulder, leaning back in a startled posture. Keeping his composure, Elton leaned forward reaching around Elaine's stiffened body to check the caller ID, which read:

Best Friend
411 Support System,
Suburb of Soul

"Wow, it's Best Friend! My number one Supporter, always with words of affirmation and encouragement!" Elton shouted excitedly as he picked up the receiver. "Hello, how are you Senior?" (That was his nickname for Best Friend.)

Best Friend responded with a big chuckle, "Hey, hello to you too, Junior." (Which was Best Friends nickname for Elton.) "So, how are you?"

"Well…," Elton paused, clearing his throat and answering with a nervous tone breaking his voice, "I… I'm well. I'm… um… sitting in my living room with a good friend." He hadn't yet told Best Friend about his progressive relationship plans with his significant other. It had been a season or two since they'd spoken, and the last thing Elton told Best Friend was about some crazy notion last New Years resolution about settling down. So he wasn't quite ready at the moment to share the big news about him and Elaine. Quickly shifting the subject, "…so, what inspired you to call me tonight Senior?"

This time Best Friend belted out a good one so loud Elton had to hold the phone away from his listening ear. "Well, buddy, you're not going to believe me when I tell you, but I called because I've been having this nagging burden for you,

Junior. Strictly business. I want to know something. Be honest with me. Were you recently rocked in your sleep and visited by Mediator? And did you happen to find... a package?"

Elton just about fell off the couch in amazement. "Uh... uh, why would you ask me that?"

"Don't worry." Best Friend reassured him. "You don't have to be afraid. I won't report you to Brother Delegator, Dictator, or any of the Elders. So tell me, is it true?"

Elaine noticing a perplexing look on his face, Elton reluctantly replied, "Yes! But... how did you know? I mean... how *could* you know?"

Best Friend waited a minute, then breathed a very heavy sigh. "I knew it. I knew this nagging burden was real. So, did you open it... and were there three books inside, one with a Swiss Army knife-pen?"

Again, "Yes!" Elton was shocked beyond reason. "How do you know these things? Were you here at the time? Did you have anything to do with putting that package and table in my bedroom?" ...as if he were talking to Santa Clause. Then with a skeptical tone, "Or is this all a big hoax or a practical joke?"

"Of course not." Best Friend distinctly reacted sharply. "That is a gift. A gift to you from Mediator. Quit avoiding and just answer my questions, Junior. Have you started reading your new book Exchanged For Life? And have you started writing in your Journey Journal?"

"Um, no. I mean... yes, I've been reading the book. But I didn't know I was supposed to start writing anything yet. I've just been waiting."

"Junior... waiting for what?" Best Friend continued with an almost demanding tone.

Elton didn't really have a good answer, nor did he know what to think about Best Friend's unusual forceful approach. But as for why... well, it just seemed obvious from his childhood teachings and to his analytical mind that anyone visited by Mediator should wait for more directions. "Well, Senior, this is all very vague to me," Elton said. "I'm not sure what I'm waiting for, but I..." then a light came on in his head, "...hey, wait a minute. Wait just one cottin' pickin' minute you rascal you. Are you yankin' my chain, Senior? Did you have a dream too you're not telling me about? Were you visited by Mediator?"

"Junior...," his friend began, trying to ignore Elton's avoidance tactics, "Well... you see, not too long ago I woke up to a similar dream too..." Best Friend kindly shared his own story with a sad tone in his voice, "...and it came with the same three books and knife-pen. It was an amazing dream, I must say. I waited and waited for about a month until one day I couldn't find my Journal and knife-pen anywhere. I searched my house but it was almost too late. Then a still small voice whispered in my ear and told me where to look. Sure enough, in the midst of difficult affections in a personal relationship, it was under my mothers Manual For Life, kept in a brief case hidden in the attic of her Perspective Home and—"

"—Hey, I haven't heard a voice in my ear..." Elton interrupted, "...and my book and pen are... well..." as Elton scurried to find them, "...they *were* right here on the end table next to the couch. Maybe I left them by my bed on the night-stand? Wait a minute while I go look upstairs—"

"NO JUNIOR," Best Friend shouted quickly. "I'll tell you *exactly* how to figure out where to find them. I know that too. First, you must think about your affections toward the one most influential person you've been trying to avoid fear, shame, guilt, and pain; probably a relationship with some significant other."

Immediately, Elton knew exactly the answer Best Friend referred to. Then he looked over at Elaine with his heart practically pounding out of his chest, put his shaky hand over the receiver, and whispered, "Crazy, I know, but do you by any chance have my Journey Journal and knife-pen?"

"Yes!" Elaine said with a surprised look on her face, pulling them out of her bag. "I was planning on giving them to you tonight. I don't remember you bringing them over, but nevertheless, you must have left them at my Perspective

Home recently. Of all places, I found yours under my copy of the Manual For Life."

"I found them." Elton spoke back into the phone, practically bewildered in a state of shock.

"Good! Remember this," Best Friend advised, "most Commoners only recall from memory ten percent of what we hear. That is why the best way to educate is to regurgitate. Make sure you write down everything as soon as possible that you can remember about your dream. Then be sure to explain it to someone else so you'll recall everything that's happened since that particular night. And also remember this, Junior..." Best Friend reiterated, "...this is your very own personal Journey Journal. It's purpose is for you to get a better grip on your Identity by tracking with your own unique story. You'll know what I mean when you go back and read it further down the road. You are to write down important things you know in your heart about who you are but were normally afraid to express out loud. Hey bud, I have to go now—"

"NO, NOT YET!" Shouted Elton. "Senior, you didn't finish telling me about your experience. What happened next?"

There was a very long pause. "Well, Junior, I think I may have forfeited my opportunity. I may have squandered it away. You see, my mother was very hard on me when she found my Journey Journal in her brief case. Underneath it was her dust-covered Manual For Life. When I went to retrieve it, I just couldn't bring myself to disappoint her, and hurt her and my dad. She was terrified when she read my sentiments in my Journal expressing my desires for more meaning and purpose in my Identity. She became so adamant about me never entertaining those urges which cause Commoners to leave Suburb of Soul and pursue their true Identity in the HeartLand. You'll know what I mean when you face the Crazy-Makers at the Border of Disorder."

Elton was sad for his friend and confused for his Self. "What the heck are Crazy-Makers?" ...he thought to himself out loud. Elaine was left in the dark

65

only hearing a one-sided conversation and trying to make sense out of his body language.

"So Junior," Best Friend added with another question, "are you going to go. You know, take the trip over the Border of Disorder, and through the Forbidden Forest, in order to go to the HeartLand in the Misty Mountains?"

"Yes I am." Elton spoke very lightly. "But please don't tell my family."

"Oh. I won't. You can count on me," Best Friend affirmed.

"Hey, maybe there's still hope for you to pursue your Big Dream! Do you want to go with me?" Elton extended the invitation.

"Oh Junior, my dear friend, please try to understand. I've been under a lot of pressure to perform at work, and in my personal life?... well, let's just say I've been far from perfect in my relationships with women, ever since the girl of my dreams slipped away. I can't really take the time to explain it right now, but I will call you again when the time is right. Although, the next time we talk, I'm sure it will most likely be time for you to go to the HeartLand and meet your Connector. So get ready and pursue your purpose with a plan for what's about to come your way. Blessings, and God bless you. Bye."

After he hung up, Elton explained the other half of the conversation to Elaine. They talked a little bit longer, and then decided to call it a night. Even though he'd always been able to rely on Best Friends support, Elton had no idea it wouldn't be until after his journey's end that he'd talk to him again.

When Elaine finished cleaning the dishes and Elton straightened things up around the living room, they expressed their final affections before wrapping up what had to be one of the most eventful, yet memorable nights of their lives, to say the least.

With his Journey Journal and knife-pen, Elton held them gently in his hands full of thoughts and questions. He too could relate to being a mama's boy like Best Friend and how that effected his difficult ability to make long term commitments. He thought about Best Friend's words, how he lost his book and knife-pen due to his relationship with his mother. "Where would Best friend be today if it wasn't for his mother's overbearing, control in his life?" he wrote on the top line of the next page in his Journey Journal.

Then, as his ears and eyes of his spirit reflected endearing thoughts, like a light bulb shining through, a surprising thought penetrated the bars of his captivated heart. Could it be that maybe Mediator visited every Commoner, especially at moments when personal relationships are most vulnerable? And could it be that Mediator gives each of them three books and a knife-pen for their journey to the HeartLand... but only *some* embraced the desire for more meaning and purpose ...and even *fewer* pursue them? Waiting too long—nearly like Best Friend did—only to lose the vision for the ultimate life exchange? Whew, such an exhausting thought. He was almost certain it was true though. He concluded that maybe, due to all the fear, shame, guilt, and pain in Best Friend's experience, which lead to rejection, there were more Commoners he knew personally who waited too long, or forfeited grace altogether?

The more he thought about Best Friend, the more he realized it was true. And a great sadness covered his face.

One thing Elton knew for sure, he wasn't about to continue making the same mistakes he'd seen in so many other Commoners from the good-Ole-boy/Old-School mentality, including his own family. He was determined more than ever not to waste another day waiting for his Identity to be fulfilled by some random chance. In this moment of vulnerability, he was determined to figure out a way to start preparing his heart before it was too late in finding his purpose.

~

More time passed. But now it didn't seem so long as Elton and Elaine were finally wed in matrimonial covenant. It was a wonderful ceremony with one simple change added to their exchanging of vows, "Til death do us Start." They were now making a life together in one commonly shared Perspective Home. Elton was more determined than ever to work hard at making his relationship with Elaine the best it could be. He wasn't going to be a *Watcher* like his father, who dictated his Perspective Home with an iron fist while his mother did all the work. Breaking the chains of bad patterns made for difficult choices. As a matter of fact, with every change came hard challenges. In so doing, humbly, he scaled down and made Self-sacrifices that were necessary so he could minimize distractions. He went back to school to get his Master degree in Counseling while working two, even three jobs at a time to pay the bills. And yet, if there was still one thing he struggled with the most, it was his lack of commitment to give complete, unconditional love to Elaine when it came to having a remnant of the wall of protection he kept to guard his heart from ever getting rejected.

Finally, one morning before worship, Elton met with another friend, Common Sense, for breakfast. Common Sense told him, "When it comes to your true Identity, don't concern yourself with the Doers. Also, don't concern yourself with all the Flesh-Modifiers, Law-Conformers, and Pselfologists. They will only hold you back. But you'll know when you're ready. You'll see it in your own eyes in the mirror of your future reflection what can only be revealed to your spirit breaking through the wall of protection around your heart. My friend, you'll never be happy and fulfilled here on this planet unless you step out of your comfort zone and completely put down your wall of protection. You were destined for more, Elton—I sense it in my spirit. But you've also got to stay off the performance-based treadmill and live according to your true Identity, which gives you freedom! Search no longer in the places of your youth. Those fantasies are gone in a child's dream world for Neverland. By putting off those childish ways, your love has changed as you're now ready for the HeartLand. Only, never return to the unhealthy faulty system targeting the soul ever again. Never return to the kind of relationships where approval is only validated by what you *do* in the eyes of other soulish Commoners. Be a Mediator pleaser, not a people pleaser."

After his exhilarating conversation full of practical advice, Elton quickly made his way to worship as a million more thoughts were swimming in his head. As soon as their eyes met, Elaine saw a certain look in his. She asked him if he'd heard back from Best Friend? He told her he hadn't and quickly changed the subject to his big plan. "I'm prepared and ready to pursue my true Identity... are you?"

Elaine concurred as she too had been planning and preparing her heart for the journey, waiting on Elton to affirm it was time to pursue the HeartLand together.

Knowing what they had to do next, Elaine had a look of concern in her eyes.

"What's the matter?" Elton asked.

"Well," Elaine said, "you act as if nothing is wrong. But you know as well as I do what all the Flesh-Modifiers and Law-Conformers among our family and friends, Preachers and Elders, even the Pselfologists are going to say once the news gets out to Local Gathering and Suburb of Soul. Everyone believes Commoners who pursue their true Identity foolishly leave and go to the HeartLand seeking silly dreams only to—"

"—Yes, yes, I know." Elton broke in. "And I can hardly wait to get started and prove them wrong!"

"So you're going to really do it?" With shrills trickling down their spines, they both heard a familiar guilt-ridden voice from behind them. It was Brother Delegator, the pulpit preacher who was a master-manipulator with all his fancy rhetoric. "I've been watching the two of you for the past month of Sundays now. Haven't you learned from past Commoners who pursued their Big Dreams while attempting to overcome an identity crisis only to return battered, bruised and rejected? Is that what you want? What you are planning to do goes completely against every value and belief you've ever been taught since birth. Elton, you are more reasonable than this. I care about who you are, but remember you have to live according to the law, which affirms your behavior as a reflection of who you are. And Elaine, you're normally more sensitive than to be so irresponsible. What happened to your loyalty and faithfulness to do what's right according to the rules and regulations. You both have so much promising potential if you'll just keep *doing* what you've been doing. Why leave your good jobs for some crazy notion about some other made-up Identity? It doesn't exist this side of heaven. How selfish can you be? Besides, you've always lived here. This is where your families are. What about your Perspective Home? You're about to throw it all away, ...and for what?"

"I've thought about all of that too," Elton spoke up, "but our Big Dream for our true Identity is real, not made-up. We finally know why we've never been able to overcome the illusion of control of the Flesh, in order to experience the passions of our hearts in the Spirit. Graciously, we were visited by the—"

"—Yeah, yeah, Mediator, who rocked you in your sleep. I've heard it all before. And you got your special books with your nifty little knife-pens, now you're ready to go on your big adventure pursuing your true Identity in the HeartLand... Blah, Blah, Blah, Blah, Blaaaah! Just a bunch of risk-taking dreamers. So you're going to become Seekers in order to exchange the old Self in Adam for a new Identity in Mediator, in order to get in touch with the new and improved YOU! Give me a break. Show me that in the Manual For Life. It's not there." Brother Delegator sarcastically mocked them.

"Oh yeah? What about Galatians 2:20? *'I have been crucified with Mdiator; and it is no longer I who live, but Mediator lives in (or through) me; and the life which I now live in the body I live by faith in the Son of Life Exchanger, who loved me and gave Himself up for me.'* Brother Delegator, we *are* Seekers with a new Identity in Mediator, so He can live His life in and through us!" Confronted Elaine. "But we still need to overcome the illusion of control in our soul, so we can learn how to think and feel with our hearts—something we can only get in the HeartLand. I'm sorry, but I don't want to be married to a good-Ole-boy/Old Schooler. I don't want Elton to turn out like you and all the rest of the macho men here in Suburb of Soul. Elton and I are destined for more!"

70

"That's right!" Elton spoke up. "Today we're putting off the old for good. Putting an end to this rut from all the letter-of-the-law programs you promote with all your spiritual disciplines you load us down with and all your hollow rhetoric, legalistic stipulations, and mediocre living within the Faulty System. You're nothing but a modern day Pharisee like the ones Mediator warned His disciples about in Matthew 23. With all due respect, all that flesh-modification is just a bunch of soulish hogwash! We're getting off the performance-based treadmill that doesn't come close to what we read about in the Manual For Life. What about the grace-based gospel that liberates us to freedom *from* being a slave to sin and *to* being righteous in Him? Plus, even though you never taught us about our need for real fellowship among believers, we want true community fellowship with other Seekers. In fact, we are leaving our regular jobs and boring routines so we can go and get prepared for our journey to the HeartLand."

And with that, Elton and Elaine walked away, singing harmoniously for the first time a new song united in the same Spirit and Truth with their hearts.

~

That night, before they each settled into their bed at their Perspective Home, Elton and Elaine eagerly examined the Manual For Life together affirming their true Identity before writing in their Journey Journals. Only, this time, with helpful reading from Exchanged For Life, they began to understand things with their heart eyes about the cross and the Life Exchanger they never acknowledged before.

Elaine held her knife-pen to her chest for a while with an attitude of gratitude, helping her intuitively remember with convictions, rather than trying to feel with her emotions, the details of her Big Dream.

But for Elton, he knew that Elaine needed to be able to rely on him as a strong leader—a man of integrity with a noble mind. So he tried to step-up acting courageous, trying to prove that he was more confident than before. He immediately started writing things down without any hesitation. Before they were to take this next step on their journey together, he would have to make an effort to implement a plan with a good strategy.

However, in spite of Elton's lifelong tendencies toward fleshly Self-efforts, Mediator intervened and guided him through the steps of charting his lifeline as well as directed his thoughts to write a very simple formula that fit every circumstance and situation:

Meaning + Purpose—with a Plan
= Fulfillment of true Identity

Chapter 3 Journey Journal

As relational human beings, people (Commoners) try desperately to find their niche in the world (Suburb of Soul) by relying on a performance-based system to determine who they are—including believers. Consider for instance that you might base your Identity on what you do for your vocation, some organization, educational institution, close relationships (i.e. a significant other, husband, wife, sports, music, good causes, games, favorite TV program, sewing, cooking, etc.), where you spend most of your time (i.e. relationships—a husband, wife, parent, grandparent, etc., job, school, hobby, investing, reading novels, video games,), a religious or cultural upbringing (i.e. Catholic, Baptist, Charismatic, Jewish, Buddhist, Islam, Italian, Asian, Hispanic, Cuban, South American, African-American, North American, Canadian, etc.), maybe your addictive flesh patterns (i.e. sex/drugs/alcohol/eating-disorder/gambling, internet), or maybe you've embraced your true Identity as a follower of Mediator who's crucified with Him on the cross and bought back by His blood (Galatians 2:20)?

Tragically, there are even faith-based leaders who've turned Mediator's commandments in Scripture (Manual For Life) into the letter of the law misunderstanding the Spirit of the law. But it is not so with those who understand their new Identity according to the new covenant: *"He has made us competent as ministers of a new covenant— not of the letter but of the Spirit; for the letter kills, but the Spirit gives life.* (2nd Cor. 3:6). That's typically why there's a quandary when people ask the question "What am I supposed to do?" …which is the worst first question most commonly asked at around this point. So let me ask you what I believe is the best first question:

Who do you believe you are?

_____

_____

_____

_____

By grace, your true "Identity" in Mediator (Christ Jesus) will help you deal with how you were once under the law (including mans laws like that of Suburb of Soul and Local Gathering). But the Truth made you free by your new identity in Mediator, which is a better covenant than the first (Gal. 3:15-29; 1ˢᵗ Tim. 2:5; Heb. 8:6; 12:24). Thus, your ultimate identity is found in Him alone who's love compels you to no longer live for your Self, but to yield your life to Him so He can live His eternal life <u>through</u> you (2ⁿᵈ Cor. 5:14).

The operative phrase is "through you." So, are you living under grace or the law? Explain your answer.

_____

_____

_____

_____

When it comes to your new Identity, it is one thing to exchange the old in order to be saved by grace for salvation (Eph. 2:8 & 9), but did you know that you are to "live by grace"? …that is called sanctification. In fact, the Bible (Manual For Life) tells us that we are to live our life the same way we received our salvation (Col. 2:6). On this journey together, we will personalize some powerful and significant truths, which show us how to live the abundant life victoriously that Mediator came to give us. We need to understand He is more than a Elton's Savior or a Commoners Crutch; He is an eternal The Life Exchanger who gives us a new Identity! Understanding who we are in Mediator is imperative to the Victorious life.

How should that affect you in your maturity from milk to meat on your everyday grace-walk journey?

_____

_____

_____

_____

Like Elton, who struggled with an illusion of control in his flesh, it's hard for followers to find our Inner Longing's meaning and purpose for true "identity" when we are doing it in our own effort (Flesh). Incidentally, you must be willing to put down your wall of protection around your heart due to how you've been conditioned in your soul. We can all learn how to think and feel with our heart only by opening up our deepest desires called our Inner Longings... even when it makes our soulish thoughts and emotions uncomfortable. When learning how to discover who you are in Mediator (who is also the eternal Tree of Life, Rev. 2:7; 22:1-5), it is vital to learn how He lives *in* and *through* your whole spirit, soul, and body.

Thus, in order for a believer to partake of the Tree of Life, is there really a difference between soul and spirit according to 1st Thes. 5:23 &24; Heb. 4:12? Yes or No. Explain your answer.

_____

_____

_____

_____

If you believe Identity is who you are at the core of your Innermost Being; put it a different way by asking two questions more personally, "What is the kind of life I have?" and "What is indicative (be a sign of, mean, manifest, reveal) of my new nature?":

_____

_____

_____

_____

As believers, we all know that at the moment we accept Christ (Mediator) as our personal savior, He comes into our heart (Col. 1:27; along with the Holy Spirit (Comforter) Eph. 3:16 & 17); but more importantly from an "Identity" perspective, we actually become a new man or new creature in Christ (1st Cor. 1:30; 2nd Cor. 5:17)

How much closer can we get to God than to be in Christ by the anointing and baptism of the Holy Spirit when we abide in Him (1st Jn. 2:27)?

_____

_____

_____

_____

Simply put, when you accepted Christ, God made you complete by His Spirit in love and freedom. He took you out of who you were in Adam—your former identity, and placed you totally in Christ—your new identity (1st Jn. 4; 1st Cor. 15:20-58). Incidentally, there are over 80 references in the New Testament using that key prepositional phrase "in Christ".

Why is the prepositional phrase "in Christ" so important to who you are?

_____

_____

_____

_____

"For you have died, and your life is hidden with Christ in God. When Christ who is our life appears, then you also will appear with Him in glory." - Colossians 3:3-4

"To me to live is Christ" – Phil. 1:21

From these verses, why is it important and why must you die in order to be made alive in Christ?

_____

_____

_____

_____

Chapter 4

From Brokenness To Wholeness

The next few months arrived with a big transition. Only, Elton woke up each day a little bit earlier than the normal, seeking and thriving with a new attitude. Then one day, unlike his normal routine, his freedom to plan and prepare for his Big Dream was interrupted. Even though he enjoyed his freedom, he still took his normal shower and ate his normal breakfast at the same time, anyway.

However, while bathing in his shower, he noticed something different about the water. Responding to this unbelievable sensation, he realized something strange was emerging from within. As he lathered his body with soap, the bar slipped right out of his hands and onto the floor beside the sink. Stepping out onto the mat to retrieve his bar of soap, he noticed there was something beyond the misty condensation on the bathroom mirror. It revealed an image requiring a deeper perception, one that he was able to somehow peer past the surface profile. With an unfamiliar distinction, it portrayed features of a face of his future Self. As he tried to look a little closer, it appeared to fit his shape perfectly. And yet, it was a reflection of a much older and wiser looking Self. As a matter of fact, it wasn't Self at all. There was a peculiar glow in his countenance as his eyes were like two portholes peering into something deep beneath the surface into a spiritual dimension. As he stared into his reflection mesmerized by the sensation, the image returned to his normal reflection and the mirror began to crackle and pop; then suddenly, shattered into a million broken pieces sustained on the wall.

Startled, he turned to shut off the running water from the shower, and then it occurred to him that Mediator provided another sign. Only this time, the image reflected in the mirror, right before the brokenness, was of the man he was always meant to be. A voice told him he needed to destroy the man he had become—just like he read in Exchanged For Life, and similar to what his friend Common Sense had told him. This was not an image showcased in a picture frame hung above the mantle. No, this portrait was captured on a canvas of misty tapestry appearing for a little while ...then it vanished away into a million pieces.

Unmistakably, there was also a blemish exposing another issue he'd been trying to avoid. But he quickly dismissed it.

Now, Elton had heard rumors of such happenings in the lives of other Commoners who'd become Followers, but the skeptical Pselfologists recorded scientific reports stating that these mystical happenings were just mere coincidences, emotional flukes, and hallucinations disguised as paranormal disturbances. Either way, once again, he had never imagined something quite as spectacular as this ever happening to him.

Hurrying to get dressed while the Passions of his heart were bursting anxiously within his chest, he wanted to share his new vision with his partner. He wanted to tell Elaine, hoping she too had a new sign from Mediator, but one without a blemish. Yet, how would he explain the broken mirror in a million pieces?

While he scurried through the house like a Lake Loon in a feeding frenzy, the phone rang—it was Common Sense.

Ring... ring... ring...

"Hello Common Sense. For some strange reason I sensed in my spirit you might be calling soon."

"How are you my dear friend? Last time we talked, I saw you talking to Brother Delegator at Local Gathering after our meeting for breakfast. He can be pretty intimidating as well as convincing. I've been hoping and praying you didn't give up on your Big Dream."

"No. I will never do that ever again."

They both laughed in a sigh of relief.

So, how is your impetuous Self?" Common Sense took control of the conversation.

"Fine…" Elton replied with a chuckle in his voice. "I really needed our talk before that Sunday for worship. I don't think I could have been so bold with Brother Delegator if it wasn't for your encouragement. I really appreciate true accountability with safe people like you more than I ever did before. In fact, it's actually great to hear your voice today at this very moment. Guess what? That moment you told me would appear in the mirror?… well, it just happened!"

"Fantastic!" Common Sense was elated to hear the news. "That's all the more reason for why I've got good news about your journey to the HeartLand. But before I tell you any of the details, I need to find out a little more about the way things are in your personal life. I want to get more acquainted with what you've been up to lately? Catch me up to speed with your family and friends, especially things between you and Elaine."

With a strange sense this was going somewhere uncomfortable, Elton said, "Well, the family's feeling fine, and I've been spending a lot of time with Elaine planning and preparing. Unfortunately, after I finished reading Exchanged For Life, I'd gotten kind of bogged down. It really hit me finally with the whole works-based gospel I'd been taught at Local Gathering my whole life. Probably in denial, and without success, I'd been trying to align my new Identity truths with some of the old policies and procedures I enjoyed in my flesh. I never realized how much control I felt when keeping the law. As you can imagine, something jolted me inside my spirit. You see, even though I now know it's unhealthy, I actually started missing the support I got from within the community of Commoners I grew up with. They all seemed to help keep me in line with all the rules. Common Sense, this might sound crude, but now I feel like I was prostituted by the performance-based system and all those godly men and women I spent my childhood looking up to. In fact, through further research, I—"

"—Wait a minute, let me get this straight," Common Sense interrupted, "remember how you used to argue with me about the letter of the law with all your systematic formulas, methods, and reasons why all those programs were needed. You'd give me all those rebuttals about why any suggestions for less organizing wouldn't work? You said people need the law to keep them in line. In fact, you were convinced that every well-greased organization has to have at least one main leader, a committee board, and all the policies and procedures to operate properly. Wow! I remember trying to point you to what's actually written in the Manual For Life about the Spirit of the law. That the only one in Kingship, Headship, Priesthood, and Chief Shepherding roll over all His Followers is Mediator, Himself. Sounds like you've done a one-eighty—finally seeing Mediator's plan for real community in the Manual For Life!"

"Yeah, that's interesting," Elton chuckled, "Brother Delegator had warned me to stay away from some of your radical ideas. He said you misinterpreted the Manual For Life and that you were out of control and didn't submit to his anointed authority. I thought about calling you a time or two, but I got buried under all the busyness as things just kept getting worse and worse. Humbly, I want you to know that I was wrong not to heed to your wisdom. I'm really sorry, Common Sense. But I'm different now. I have a much greater respect for how you've always directed me back to the Manual For Life, rather than just give me your opinion. In fact, I have some other things I want to get your insights about since I've had to realize you're on the right track after all. Can we start with the good stuff first, if you don't mind? You see... I need some help dealing with Elaine's mom and dad—"

"Sure... of course..." Common Sense interrupted. "I know Elaine's mom, Embellisher. She's been all over the map with her emotional feel-good faith with very little substance in the Manual For Life. (Common Sense was blunt that way.) As a matter of fact, she's been a part of a variety of Local Gatherings throughout the South. And Elaine's good-Ole-boy dad, Story-Teller, was a young up-n-comer for the police force as an amazing detective of domestic affairs. An excellent officer, but not much of a dad. Poor Elaine, I've always felt sorry for her. Is that what's part of the problem?"

"Well, I'm not sure what the problem is. Listen, I know everyone is entitled to their own opinion, but when it comes to marriage and family, I'm really discouraged about Elaine's wishy-washiness when she's around her family. It's like she's a totally different person still trying to please them in her flesh, almost as if she still needs their approval and acceptance, and then she's like a totally different person with me."

"Oh, I see... you're worried they might try to persuade Elaine not to go to the HeartLand?"

"I think we're beyond that..." Elton searched for the right words. "In fact, it's way more than... well, to be honest with you, and please don't judge me, we recently encountered a problem with all of her family, including her aunt and uncle. I basically told Elaine to make a choice, it was either me or them, but—"

"—What! Hold the phone! Shut the front door! You did what? Woooow! That's pretty bold... and forgive my saying it, but maybe a bit stupid—if I might add? I can only imagine...," Common Sense chuckled out loud, "...how's married life treating you *now*?" Common Sense continued chuckling sarcastically.

"Yeah, rub it in. I guess I had that one coming. To be honest, it's not so good. Heck, it's a big mess! In fact, the whole *becoming-one* thing's got me kinda confused whenever I try to take the initiative as the leader in our relationship."

"Yeah, umm, wait a minute my friend." Common Sense interrupted again. "Sounds to me like your back in your flesh again. Let me ask you something about your leadership role in your marriage… are you still holding on to some of your good-Ole-boy/Old-Schooler mentality?"

"What do you mean?"

'Well, those mentalities of the flesh in the faulty cultural system treat women and children as if men have the right to act like the boss-man in their own Perspective Homes. That does not fly with the Manual For Life!"

Elton pondered on the sobering thought. "You're probably right. That's probably why my approach with her reminds her of the men in her family. It only gets me in the doghouse labeled Control Freak—and you know why I hate that label. But I still can't figure out why one minute we get along great in our own Perspective Home, and then Elaine gets that people-pleaser, guilt-trip demeanor when she's around her family and friends. Oh, and then she's all mad at me if I try to point this out to her about being phony or superficial."

"Sounds to me like you have a lot of anger you take out on her."

"Ouch. Thanks a lot, friend. Now it sounds like you're taking up her defense."

"Does she need defending?" Common Sense quickly returned foolish reasoning with a cutting bite of wisdom.

"That's another thing I hate. It's the way her family and friends are always taking up her defense and not encouraging her to stand up for herself, in a healthy way!"

"Why do you think it's that way?"

"I don't know, but I can't stand the way she's always trying to accommodate everyone else like sweet-little-Elaine, but never takes a stand with me or on my behalf when it's appropriate."

"Oh, so you think what's appropriate is that she should fight your battles for you."

"Now you sound like her. No. That's not what I mean at all!" Elton felt like hanging up the phone.

Sensing the tension, Common Sense quickly jumped in, "Look man, you and I have been good friends a long time. I get the impression you think you've made a mistake. Do you?"

"Sometimes I do," Elton said, finally getting it off his chest. "It sometimes feels like a hopeless cause, especially if any of our beliefs and values differs with her family—they treat her like she's not capable of thinking for herself and just walk all over her when I'm not around. Whenever I try to step in taking the initiative to express my opinion—even if it might ruffle a few feathers—she blames me for having a big mouth! But *never* does she stand up to her parents whenever she's with me, especially whenever anyone comes against me. She avoids conflict like a plague. All she cares about is keeping the peace, no matter the cost, even if it costs me my respect for her. But even the Manual For Life makes it clear that two are stronger than one against their opposition. I just can't figure out why she won't partner with me whenever others are acting like jerks, especially her family?" Elton rambled on in his pity party.

"Hmmm... I think I'm getting a better picture now. I know it can't be easy, Elton, but what has this done to the quality of your relationship, especially the intimacy?" Common Sense spoke as a seasoned mediator in relational disputes.

"I'm not sure *what* we are because there are so many thoughts and feelings of shame and guilt coming from her family, causing us both a lot of stress! I can't figure it out. As for the intimacy... what intimacy? All I know is—"

"—What seems to be the real problem, Elton?" Common Sense interrupted again in his active-listening style, "You seem tense and uptight about something more than you're telling me. My inner radar has always been able to pick up when you're overwhelmed with anxiety from fear and shame—almost panicky in the tone of your voice. One thing about you, you're stoic Old-School mentality has never been comfortable with the *vulnerability* of accountability, while your flesh tries to be in control. If my memory serves me correct, there are times you don't mind talking about your emotions, but, boy, if you're anything like you used to be, you sure don't like feeling them in front of others. About the only emotion your comfortable showing is your anger when you feel misunderstood or unappreciated. I bet you're having those sleep depravations again, aren't you?"

"Is it that obvious?" Elton felt a little psychoanalyzed and way too exposed. "Yea, my sleeping is a problem right now. But that's not all, I have anxiety issues going on too. Well, anyway, after a lot of serious thought and consideration, I've realized that people have noticed I have a problem with my attitude toward Elaine. When it comes to intimacy in our relationship, sometimes I'll avoid it by getting real busy. You know… the whole avoidance thing to protect my heart from getting hurt. The unconditional love thing, along with the physical issues also seems to keep me loaded down with shame. Incredibly, those reoccurring issues I'm still struggling with from the past are the whole reason why things always seem to creep into my personal and professional life. To be completely honest, that's why I'm seeking your advice about the *Heart Connection* and the *Fair Exchange* thing you and Kindred-Spirit like to talk about. But don't forget, at least I'm still trying to work things out with *my* wife. Heck, ever since you went through your melt down over your divorce, you haven't been completely the same."

Common Sense knew Elton resorted to a very mean, passive aggressive jab as a defensive mechanism to justify his own situation. And yet, with pride swelling in his flesh, Common Sense immediately cried out to Comforter in his spirit to defuse the anger and hurt he was feeling. Elton just cut him deep. He asked Life Exchanger for the compassion needed to forgive and overlook this offense. At this pivotal moment, he experienced a peace that surpassed all understanding, just when things could have been absolutely disastrous for both of them. Instead, Common Sense regained his composure with a wise response.

"Elton, as best as you can, in your own words, help me understand what you're experiencing on the inside. Is there a movie, lyrics to a song, or a story from the Manual For Life that can help you give me a word picture or illustration to what things look like from your perspective."

"Ok," Elton liked this approach, "remember how we took that computer class together in college? Don't you think it would be so much easier if we were wired like computers? If we were, I'd explain it to you this way: I've finally decided to install extra gigs of ram for Love and Grace on my hard drive in order to get Peace of Mind programmed into my software. In fact, I want to know more about adding the Inner Longings component. I think I need a kind of Network System that comes from Accountability shareware. I've decided that I want to experience a connection with Elaine that requires me to remove my wall of protection from rejection. I don't know if that helps, but that's the best I can come up with."

"Hmm…" Common Sense pondered, as he knew his friend's tendencies were stuck in a fleshly mind set. "So… you're still hiding behind that computer lingo, aren't you? Well, first of all, it's not an easy process getting unplugged from the matrix of the Faulty System—especially since you've been conditioned for so long. Secondly, your intangible spirit is not exactly like a physical hard drive or motherboard in a computer. But I do know where you're coming from."

"Ok, so what do I need?"

"Well, Elton, first thing is you look at the manual. In this case, your solutions are based on the Manual For Life. And according to it, you don't need more software, gigs of ram, or an additional component. Because you're a believer, what you need, you already have? That all came with the original package. Unfortunately, you've got a lot of clutter on your flesh monitor that needs to be removed. For Commoners, this process is called Brokenness. But, it sounds like what you might be missing is learning how to activate your True Identity regularly. As difficult as it might seem at times, you must stay focused and determined to destroy your old identity completely. That's the first most important part. Once you've exchanged your old identity for the new one, True Identity needs to be activated by the Comforter on a daily basis. But, let me ask you this, is your heart shut down right now with a wall of protection around it? …and before you answer that, let me ask you another question, are you sure you're prepared for this revolutionizing change in your life?"

"Yes. I'm sure. Come on man, I wouldn't be asking if I wasn't serious about this."

"Ok, I was just making sure you've counted the cost. Please try to understand when I say, you have to completely erase and remove your old software. You have to get rid of all the fleshly junk from the Faulty System programmed in your mind, will, and emotions of your soulish hard drive. You see, if you don't want anymore of those nasty viruses you got from the performance-based system, exchanging the old for the new is almost like changing from a PC to a Mac. You're now operating from a new standard for processing information. It requires a lot more on the front end in order to get the best return on your investment in the long run. Basically, what I mean is that you must exchange the old stinkin-thinkin for a new right-believing from a heart perspective according to the Manual For Life."

"Yes..." Elton projected with an edge to his response before Common Sense could continue. "...to answer your question again, I'm more than ready. I can't get Elaine out of my head twenty-four seven, even though sometimes we get cross connections and she gets on my nerves. But I want this to work."

"Whoa. Ok. Let's see... you said after a lot of serious thought and consideration... um... most Thinkers like yourself usually turn to Self-help books for personal problems like these. What is it exactly that caused you to consider opening up to me after all this time rather than a Pselfologist?"

"Well, actually..." Elton interjected, "I tried going to a Pselfologist after Brother Delegator assigned one to me on staff. But he didn't even attempt to deal with my spiritual issues, especially according to the Manual For Life. I felt like a lab rat in a maze being conditioned to think, feel, and behave according to a bunch of propaganda. Relationally, I'm just as confused as ever in my life. I know that my problems are deeper than just mental and emotional. I won't lie, being in a relationship with Elaine and her family challenges me at the core of my faith—not just physically and emotionally. Common Sense, even though I have to admit she's the right one for me, still, we're also very different, almost extreme opposites... in the natural sense—if you know what I mean? The only thing we have going for us is that we're great in bed ...that is, whenever we get intimate, which isn't a whole lot lately. Undeniably, I really do have deep feelings stirring inside me that I've never had before. But, my mom says I just need to bite the bullet and accept our gender differences along with our family background differences. My dad, Control Freak, has all of a sudden taken a more passive backseat approach. Says he'll support whatever I decide."

"That's a new one." Common Sense said sarcastically.

"Yeah, I know." Elton continued, "But any way, Elaine says I'm too private about my heart—like I'm holding on to something that keeps me from being thankful and appreciative toward her. It's really odd, even though she can tell something's bothering me, she doesn't see how her constant efforts to be one person for me and another for her family only sends me packing—emotionally that is. I just want her to be confident in her own skin and share life with me her way, not worrying about what everyone else thinks ...including me. I don't want her to change and try to be someone other than who she really is. But, heck, I'm not sure she knows who she really is, and that makes it hard for me to love her for who she is. It's as though she's relying on everyone else's approval and acceptance to validate her Identity's worth and value. I hate to say it, but all that codependency needy stuff makes my skin crawl. And yet, at the same time, in spite of all our major differences, I don't know how, but she can still read me like a book. Common Sense, you'd think all women had the same gift of intuition." Elton paused... "And get this, she even says I have a tendency to be too reserved with my personal thoughts and feelings about something in the past, but she just can't put her finger on it."

"Well, is there?"

"Is there what?"

"Come on Elton… is there something you're holding on to as a secret from the past?"

"Yeah, but I don't want her to know that. I already told you a while ago. Remember when you tried to sell me on something I needed to do, something about my feelings?"

"Ok, now I know you're full of bull. Be straight with me, Elton. What the heck are you talking about? I'm not a mind reader and I don't have a crystal ball," Common Sense remarked while losing his patience.

"You know, the way I used to play a lot of head-games in college with girls in order to avoid feeling insecure. I thought I moved on from all that until I got married. So what am I supposed to do about it in this situation?"

"Well, first of all, I wouldn't say I was trying to sell you on anything…," Common Sense, a little irritated, tried to keep things on track, "…but remember what we've talked about before, solving your problems doesn't begin with what you need to *do*. As a matter of fact, that's the first worst question most people ask due to all the performance-based teaching out there. Let me remind you, that's not who you are anymore as a follower of Mediator. And second, it's really not about thoughts and feelings either. The human spirit is all about *being*, according to your new nature, in your true Identity. You can only *be* who you really *are* according to the condition of your Innermost Being. You see, Elton, because you're a Human Being rather than a Human Doer, who you *are* should make the difference in what you do. You have to begin with your heart in order to effect what you think and feel from an inside-out perspective. However, I can see that the way you still think, feel and act right now is actually dictating what you're doing in your flesh. That's because your soul is in control. Ironically, you're missing the most important point of the Manual For Life."

"You're reminding now of my Connector, Kindred-Spirit. You're starting to talk in riddles. Just keep it simple for me."

"Perhaps you'll understand it this way. As human beings, we don't always *do* with our thoughts and feelings on the outside what we know and believe on the inside. Often times, we're not thinking and feeling with our heart—especially us men!"

Elton's eyebrows rose as the expression on his face reflected the strings of his heart.

Common Sense continued, "Having tracked with you pretty closely over the years, Elton, you still probably get offended and take things way too personally when others question your motives based on your actions… almost like attacking your character, right?"

Elton tried hard to fly under the radar but he knew he was dealing with an expert who had his number.

"Yeah. Guilty as charged."

Common Sense added to his point, "Elaine probably says things like, '*if* you really love me, you wouldn't treat me that way.' But, believe it or not, that's all about those fleshly illusions of control in the soul. And yet, it gets even more complicated than that at a deeper level. According to the Manual For Life, it's really all about the third-dimension of your heart, which, as you know, is spiritual in nature. But let's go with the computer lingo since that's what you're able to relate to for now. Funny, but word pictures like that seems to work for most Commoners like you a lot better than the charts and graphs for other objective thinkers. So listen… let me walk you through the steps to freedom processing love and grace as if you're installing a new program into your computer. As you know, the first step is to reboot and click on Start and open your Control Panel. Next you go to Add or Remove Programs."

"Yes, I know all that," Elton interrupted, "but there are several other programs running through my mind right now. Is it okay to install Love and Grace while they're spinning around in my head?"

"Wait! What programs are running through your mind right now?"

"Let's see...," Elton contemplated where this conversation was headed, "well, I really didn't want to have to explain this part if I didn't have to right now. Umm, you see, I recently put someone else in jeopardy with a virus I think I passed on to them with a flash drive from a bad web site I was on a few months ago. Plus, I have a menu full of Past Hurt, Rejection, Fear, Depression, Low Self-esteem, Guilt, and Confusion all running at the same time. I've completely lost my Joy and Peace."

"Whoa! That might explain some things...," Common Sense confirmed. "From what you told me earlier, you're downloaded with all kinds of burdens, which lead to a lot of secret escapes and coping mechanisms in cyberspace fantasies. But, in order to program Brokenness into your system, you have to activate the Love and Grace software. It comes with Joy, Peace, Thankfulness, and Forgiveness. Along with these, what you'll also need to program into your system is Attitude Of Gratitude, which will gradually erase Past Hurt and Rejection from your operating system. They may remain in your permanent memory, though, but will no longer disrupt or corrupt other programs as long as you prohibit the Illusions of Control and activate Forgiveness and Joy every day. That's what gets rid of Guilt, Shame and Confusion along with the virus from that bad web site. True Identity will eventually override Low Self-esteem and Depression with a module of its own called Optimum True Identity. However, Elton, I'm here to tell you, your biggest problem is Fear. That's the worse kind of virus preventing Trust from being properly installed and makes your system very slow and susceptible to other viruses like Illusion of Control. Did you hear me? ... Illusion of Control. You need to revoke that. Unsuspectingly, if you're not aware, deeds of Self-righteousness override True Identity and your Motherboard (which is what I'm referring to as the spiritual nature of your Heart) will shut down. Elton, can you see how that's the cause for the Hardened Wall of Protection around your Motherboard, which in effect, shuts down good memories on your Hard Drive? You need an emotional Fire-Wall to guard your system from all those confusing feelings that freeze you up. Sounds strange, like an oxymoron, I know. Most men say this all sounds like a foreign language at this point, but can you turn those off first, before going any further?"

"I don't know how to turn them off emotions once they've taken control. All I've ever known is how to keep them from happening in the first place. Heck, once this happens, I'm completely at a loss for any strategy. Can you tell me how?" Elton asked with frustration in his voice.

"Absolutely. You must be patient, though. I hope you're writing all this down in your Journey Journal because you'll have to go over this multiple times for a while. First, go to your start menu and invoke Forgiveness. Do this as many times as necessary until Guilt and Confusion have been completely erased."

"Okay, done!" Elton said. "Love and Grace have started installing… is that normal?"

"Yes…" Common Sense jumped in again, "…ok, but remember that you only have the basic program. You'll need to connect to other Network Providers in order to get the upgrades from who we call Safe Accountability Partners."

"Oops! I have an error message already saying, Program Cannot Run On External Components. What should I do?"

"Don't worry, Elton. You're not going to rely on External Components any-more. It's all Internal from here on out. Basically, that means the Love and Grace program is set up to run only on the Internal Heart Connection, but has not yet been run on your Heart—or Motherboard… as you like to call it. In non-technical terms, it simply means you have to accept the Love for your own value and worth before you can actually love others the way they're intended to be loved. Next, notice a need for Reconciliation in order for a complete restoration of Trust can run on your Heart-Connections program."

"So, now what?"

Common Sense was on a roll as there seemed to be a method to his mad-ness. "Ok, pull down the Acceptance program that is part of True Identity;

then click on the following files: Forgive-Your-Past; Realize-Your-Worth; and Acknowledge-Your-Limitations.

"Okay, done," Elton said.

"Now, copy them to your My New Nature directory. The system will over-write any conflicting files from Self-Centered Identity and begin patching any faulty programming fragmented throughout your system. Also, you need to delete Self-Criticism from all directories and empty your Recycle Bin to make sure it is completely gone, never to come back again. Remember to click on the Saved Assurance button frequently.

"Got it. Hey! My hard drive is filling up with new files. Smile is playing on my monitor. Peace, Joy and Contentment are copying all over my New Nature. Thankfulness is downloading Attitude of Gratitude. Is this normal?"

"Yes. Excellent! But Elton, I'm surprised in your case that you're system is accepting this so well so soon! Must be from all the time you've been spending in the Manual For Life. Remember, for others who've been badly damaged and haven't spent nearly as much time in the Word, it can take quite a bit longer. Eventually, everyone who is willing to plug into Healthy System gets it at the proper time. So... back to the set up... Love and Grace is now installed and running freely on Law of Liberty. One more thing before we talk about your Journey to the HeartLand. Love and Grace is what's called Freeware. Be sure to give it to Elaine and any friends and family so you can share the Exchanged For Life principles with them, if their hearts are open and willing with the Fair Exchange program. Also, let me remind you, this is only the start of New Beginnings. If you want this to last, you must go through the whole journey crossing the Border of Disorder, find the path to Forbidden Forest into the Wilderness, then to the HeartLand. The rest of your *quest* for more meaning and purpose will come together when you and Elaine meet up with your Connector. I'll fill you in more about that later. Now, let's talk about the Journey to the HeartLand. There are some very important things I need to warn you about first...

~

After Elton and Common Sense finished discussing the details about leaving for the HeartLand, Elton hung up the phone and sat out on the deck for a while. Now, as a learning Seeker with new steps to freedom running through his heart and soul, it occurred to his Self, from now on, he needed to be more careful and wiser in the decisions he was making with Elaine. Like his friend, Common Sense, his knowledge and understanding were to be harnessed in the wisdom from the Manual For Life showcased in their new Perspective Home. He was to never again prematurely offer his precious jewels to any soulish Commoners who are living according to the faulty system. But first, he needed an attitude adjustment, especially when it came to brokenness. He had to quit resisting the Refiner's fire when things get a little too hot for his comfort zone.

Normally stoic and private with his personal feelings, Elton was depressed for the first time in a very long time—if maybe for the very first time. Without having eyes to see at the time—and not that long ago—his blemish had to do with a pleasureful feeling that tempted him to give into an invitation to have dinner with a Commoner named Flattery. With all her smooth enticing words stroking his ego, it reminded him of his youthful fantasies feeding his flesh. Next, as bad company corrupts good morals, it was Popularity and then Success who all became subtle pitfalls to his values and beliefs. Elton allowed his ego to seek validation in all the wrong places. Consequently, due to the guilt and shame that followed, he shut down and wore a mask on the outside, hiding all the hurt and confusion on the inside, which made him vulnerable to the Flesh-Modifiers and Law-Conformers.

Unfortunately, this was a big part of the secret Elton had been avoiding for a while. He was starting to feel completely stuck and defeated while considering more old flesh patterns. He realized he was facing a dilemma about telling Elaine the truth about the past. As a matter of fact, he gave in to some of the soulish reasons behind asking her to marry him—knowing he really wasn't unconditionally in love with her at the time. Spilling his guts could possibly jeopardize their already fragile relationship. Elton was afraid of disapproval and abandonment from Elaine and others would hold this against him for the rest of his life. He couldn't afford anymore rejection. He just wanted to keep it all in and crawl under a rock on another planet in some other galaxy. Out of a state of reclusive withdrawal from all his childhood issues, Elton now realized what had really happened back at a time he was most vulnerable. Once he built a thick protective wall around his heart, his fear of rejection never went away. Now, his most recent mistake was like the icing on the cake. Those who'd find out about Flattery and all her foolish friends, especially from the good-Ole-boy/Old Schooler social network—they were the ones who would use his mistakes against him conveniently when the time was right.

Defensively, out of avoidance, he withdrew his reliance on all his good friends like Common Sense, due to those who indulged his wrong motives. Relying on those he thought he could trust in the faith, they were the ones who practically chewed him up and spit him out the worse in the flesh. No grace... only guilt. Due to the rumors spread among Local Gatherings, he'd been wounded deeply by a few pulpit Preachers in Suburb of Soul accusing him of lies along with all those who completely abandoned him in the ministry. If they knew about this, he might as well shoot himself in the head. Consequently, shut down on the inside, Elton had become reserved with his thoughts and feelings disconnected from his heart due to all the fear, shame, guilt, and pain that led to rejection.

But now, Elaine needed to know the decisions Elton was making before they began their new journey together. She wanted a covenant commitment from his heart and not just a contract with his soul.

After a while, flip-flopping like a fish on a chopping block, he began to switch from frustration to resentment, then back to anger and bitterness all over again. All the same doubts and fears from the past flooded his mind questioning maybe he didn't really receive a Big Dream from Mediator. And maybe his personal relationship with Mediator wasn't really real at all. Maybe the Pselfologists were right, his ideas were merely delusional crazy notions and hallucinations conjured up in his head. Oh the temptation to harden his heart was stronger than ever.

In a moment of despair, he ran back to the bathroom and turned on the hot water for steam, but all he saw was a reflection of Old-Self in the broken mirror with depression on his face.

After loneliness had just about taken its toll, one evening after dinner, Elton was consumed with remorse and sorrow. He went to his study to read his Manual For Life hoping that Mediator would communicate something new. He wrote in his Journey Journal, but nothing was helping.

Elaine knew something was obviously very wrong for quite some time, as she could sense it deep inside her intuitive radar system. Without permission, she attempted to comfort the tender heart she so dearly loved. As Elton and Elaine sat in the darkness of silence, neither knew what to say. But it was her meek and mild manner driven by mercy and compassion that brought comfort without words.

Elton just couldn't bring himself to tell Elaine all the shameful stuff that had happened in the past. His emotions just couldn't bear the anxiety of disappointment that his words might grieve her spirit. If he told her the truth, the whole truth, and nothing but the truth—so help him God—she might think everything about him and their relationship was one big lie.

But that was not the truth about *her* character. Elaine placed her hands on his face, gave a squeeze to his lips... then spoke these words. "I love you Elton no matter what it is that you're going through. Please don't block me out. Just let me love you even when you're unsure about loving me or ...yourself. But remember this, you're not alone. We're in this together. I believe in you and I know you'll make the right decisions for our future. I know I sometimes frustrate you with all my insecurities and issues in my flesh. But do not fill your cup with the wrong thing, even if that means we both must be empty for a while. We'll be

Ok. I trust the motives and intent inside your heart even though at times you've made bad decisions in your flesh on the outside. Don't forget, we've both come so far through so much. Elton, I heard from Mediator again. The Comforter showed me another vision while I was taking a shower. With depth perception, I was able to see past the surface and I saw your future face in the broken mirror. This time Mediator spoke to me while I was reading my Manual For Life and praying for you. I also received a call from Kindred-Spirit. He told me that it's time to leave for the HeartLand. Along with my personal pursuit, part of my responsibility is to love and support you... no matter what! The last thing the Comforter said to me was, "Fear not... I will provide all your needs for you and be with you wherever you go."

A peace came over his whole body and soul pouring out from within his spirit. Elton was relieved from the fear and anxiety about sharing his past with Elaine. Finally the breaking point brought him to brokenness and brought about wholeness. He opened up his heart with her, and she with him, in renewed hope. He was more confident than ever that she forgave him before he even spoke one word.

And with that, Mediator healed Elton and Elaine and they were reconciled, resolved and restored in their hearts and minds not knowing this was all part of Mediator's plan for Brokenness leading to Wholeness.

A thought occurred to Elton as he was writing in his Journey Journal that night: spiritual brokenness is the process every Commoner needs to go through in order to break free, which leads to Wholeness from Mediator's ultimate sacrifice on the cross.

They were now prepared to venture out on their journey to the HeartLand.

Chapter 4 Journey Journal

Like Elton and Elaine, we need to put our journey into perspective, so let's take a look at our own need for Brokenness that leads to Wholeness. We need to understand what really happened to the common man's nature when Adam chose to disobey God if we are to understand why our flesh patterns must be broken at a spiritual level.

In the Beginning, our spirit-life (Zoë) became spiritually dead or dormant <u>to</u> God immediately at the fall. Consequently, our fellowship was broken <u>with</u> God and our eternal condition became death. As a tri-part being with spirit, soul, & body, Adam (and consequently us because we inherited the sin nature from Adam – Romans 5:19) was left dysfunctional with only 2 of 3 life resources—soul-life (psuche) and body-life (bios). In the Flesh, Adam was on his own to cope with life in order to get his needs met apart from God. We also, therefore, apart from Christ, could only live by the flesh—or sin nature (2nd Cor. 5:16).

Before Christ (because of our inheritance in Adam) our sin nature developed what the Bible calls flesh patterns (coping mechanisms) to get our soulish and physical needs met independent from God. These coping mechanisms were developed and conditioned from childhood. Some are developed after childhood or even after our salvation, but certainly many have continued in our Christian life without breaking free from the patterns of the world spoken of in 2nd Cor. 5:17.

For Example, when you find yourself struggling with your flesh patterns: Who or what do you try to get your <u>primary</u> needs of love and acceptance met thru?

_____

_____

_____

_____

Who or what do you try to get your <u>primary</u> needs of value and appreciation met thru?

_____

_____

_____

_____

Where do you spend most of your efforts trying to get your <u>primary</u> needs met?

_____

_____

_____

_____

Recognize this pattern:

- **Relationships** (parents/siblings/family/teachers/friends/church/ spouses):

  ⮕ Create circumstances.....

- **Circumstances** (social, school, work, cultural, home, drama/divorce/traumas):

  ⮕ Trigger thoughts & emotions......

- **Thoughts & Emotions** (validation/affirmation; fear-shame-guilt-pain=rejection):

  ⮕ Internalize fleshly perspective (which becomes our reality).....

- **Internalize Fleshly Perspective** (effect point of view, beliefs, values, morals)

  ⮕ Bad choices in behavior

- **Bad Choices in Behavior** (talk too much, shut down, build a wall around heart)

  Survival coping mechanisms and flesh-patterns.

So what are the meanings of the word "flesh" or "flesh-patterns"?

In the Greek there is only one word that is translated flesh and it is the word *sarx*. There are many contexts for the use of that word however:

Luke 24:39	skin and other soft parts of body
1st Peter 4:1	body as a whole
John 6:53-56	allegory
Galatians 5:19-21	deeds/actions
Romans 8:8, 12, 13	ways of spiritual living and attempting to get our needs met

Note: There is only one Greek word depicting "sin nature" in humans and that is "sinner" (hamartolos), which is our condition before Christ. However, after Christ, the word depicting "sin nature" in a believer's life is the word for flesh (*sarx*).

So, you need to identify your flesh by writing down your honest thoughts about your own flesh patterns.

a.   What is it about your flesh that wants to be in *control* (of circumstances, of outcomes, of pleasure, in answering to God on your terms, in *protecting* your heart with a wall)?

_____

_____

_____

_____

b. In what ways is it hard for you to accept that the flesh will profit you nothing? (John 6:63)

_____

_____

_____

_____

c. As anger builds, loneliness sets in. In what ways have you become angry with God? (Romans 8:7)

_____

_____

_____

_____

d. Why do you struggle at times accepting nothing good dwells within your flesh? (Romans 7:17)

_____

_____

_____

_____

e. If flesh produces death (Romans 8:13), what weakness keeps your eyes blind to the solution?

_____

_____

_____

_____

f. Knowing there is no eternal value in the flesh (John 15:5), what are you holding on to on earth?

_____

_____

_____

_____

g. We all try to justify our flesh through Self-righteous deeds (Phil 3:9), what are some of yours?

_____

_____

_____

_____

Note to (g.): *Setting Self-made standards for others to meet your expectations, or trying to meet unrealistic Self-made standards for your Self is "legalism" and "manipulation." Setting lofty standards for oneself is Self-righteousness – basically whoever sets an unrealistic standard for themselves that they didn't think they could keep, which is sabotage?*

Chapter 5

Overcoming The Illusion Of Light

N ot knowing the details of their far off future, Elton and Elaine wanted to focus on the immediate needs for that day. And yet, unbeknownst to them, there were a couple of things that still needed to be dealt with between them.

Like planning for a vacation, on the agenda was getting their Perspective Home in order, making a list, then packing their bags in the truck, putting supplies on the trailer, and lastly, heading out of town.

So much to do in so little time.

From his vantage point, Elton needed all the *leverage* he could find to keep his pioneering momentum moving forward so that he wouldn't get distracted from all the thoughts and feelings he'd already overcome.

But there was still the blemish.

His hyper sensitive conscience became like a tiller bogging down in mud. It was relatively easy for him to get stuck in his flesh while plowing raw fields of emotions in his soul. Nothing seemed to help but get busy and stay busy.

The day for departure finally arrived. After their house was in order, and just before Elton's bags were fully packed on the truck, a thought kept stirring in his mind as he was about to fasten his personal suitcase shut. One of the very last things Common Sense said about traveling to the HeartLand was to guard their heart from footholds and strongholds. *"Footholds & Strongholds depend on what you're holding on to,"* is all he said. In this case, he was referring to the Crazy-Makers. They were the ones waiting at a rickety old Bridge crossing the Raging River—which marked the Border of Disorder.

An extra detail without a generous response. That was it. No other facts. No solution was given. Nothing else discussed. All that Common Sense offered was a hefty warning that *couldn't* be mistaken.

Suddenly, feeling the need for a good strategic implementation of his plan, Elton reworked his purpose with a plan. He took out his Journey Journal and wrote out a plan-of-action right next to his to-do-list along with the tid-bits from everyone's wise advice. From his business sense, Elton called this plan the SWOT SPOT, and made an Inspection Check-List for his immediate situation.

Soon, Elton and Elaine were driving away from the comfort and familiarity of their Perspective Home in Suburb of Soul. They drove past the county line and then toward the part of town most Commoners tried to avoid called the Border of Disorder—better known as the place where Crazy-Makers try to drive you insane.

These survivors had never even considered venturing this far away, especially across town to the Border of Disorder. The only adventures that they enjoyed were camping and four-wheeling in the nearby northern mountain ranges. They both knew that the farther they traveled from Suburb of Soul the less familiar they'd be with other Commoners, especially those whom they'd known their whole life, including family. It was part of the cost of pursuing their Inner Longing's Big Dream for more meaning and purpose.

Right on the border, they were to look for a bridge crossing over the Raging River. There, Commoners are said to have been overcome by a mysterious light while taking the Big Risk with a leap of faith. Anyone who would dare leave their comfort zone was considered delusional by the Pselfologists unless they returned immediately to normal thoughts and feelings they left behind. Those who returned did so due to fear, shame, guilt, and pain, which left everyone's Self feeling the most dreaded feelings of all—loneliness from rejection! This could only add more layers to the already existing wall around their hearts.

Some were so glad when they got back, they plugged their souls back into their boxes at their Perspective Homes for weeks and even months, escaping into a sense of relief while waiting for their Inner Longings to fade into oblivion.

But Elton and Elaine told each other they were different from most Commoners in Suburb of Soul. They would pursue their Big Dream no matter what it would take. And whenever they did return, they would be better for it and share their adventure with all their friends and family at Local Gathering.

Foreseeing only good in the future, they stayed the course. While approaching the bridge over the Raging River from a distance, they were determined not to get distracted. They focused on their Inner Longings by singing together their new song in harmony. Life had never seemed so promising.

And then, something happened.

The hopeful anticipations in their spirits did not last long. They both subtly lost their focus. When they were no longer singing their melodious tune, Elaine couldn't say why, but she just wasn't feeling the mood anymore. Like a fleeting thought, Elton couldn't explain why, but he just wasn't in the same frame of mind for some odd reason. Then as they began to travel a little bit farther toward the bridge, they both began to have some of those old soulish thoughts and feelings toward each other that were uncomfortably awkward.

Next thing they knew, Elaine was no longer in the middle of the front seat sitting next to Elton, she had moved away near the passenger door where she felt safer for some strange reason. With a classic Archie Bunker pious confidence, "*I'm not the one who moved,*" Elton remained steady while holding tightly to the steering wheel. The scenery looked different. There was an eerie tint of orangey-greenish light reflected on the trees and fields as there were ominous clouds hovering all around them.

Elton, keeping his thoughts to his Self, Elaine, keeping her feelings to her Self, both reconsidered their pursuit for their Big Dream. For the first time, it was becoming apparent that processing their thoughts and feeling with their heart could cause a deeper discomfort than normal. All their thoughts and feelings looked different from their current perspective dealing with their circumstances. It was true: what they had back in Suburb of Soul was *good*! But in order to seek the *best* in the HeartLand, good would become the enemy of best. In fact, it also occurred to them that in order to go from good to best, things had to go from bad to worse! There was a tug of war in their flesh seeking control between their heart and soul.

The difficulty of these thoughts and feelings were excruciatingly painful as the light they'd embraced about their new beliefs was now becoming dim with an illusion of control in their soul. They didn't know what to do about their failing faith in the midst of their latest identity crisis. They began to wonder who they are all over again …or who they really ever were? They would have to interact with unfamiliar Commoners in unfamiliar places. They wouldn't have their familiar Perspective Home to come back to every day or worship every Sunday at Local Gathering with family and friends.

Startled by the horror of it all, Elton intently looked at Elaine with an even more disturbing thought: to pursue what he most desired… he would have to face what he most dreaded! "What happened to their reconciliation?" he wondered.

Elton's thoughts were interrupted by intruding emotions that caused a very anxious moment. He pulled over and put the truck in neutral. He began to have big doubts about pursuing his Inner Longings. What was he thinking? What did it all mean? He doubted that he had any natural gifts, talents, or abilities to succeed at his ambitions. Fearful feelings told him that most of his endeavors were from acquired skills at the aid of others. Plus, he was clearly inadequate to love and cherish his partner's qualities when she obviously didn't meet his unrealistic expectations. In fact, despite his commitment to their covenant, there were times he didn't even think he liked her. How could he ever *really* love, trust, and respect Elaine, let alone accept and openly share in a Fair Exchange? What if he failed right in front of other Commoners? What would that do to his reputation—or do to his beliefs and values due to his preconceived notions?

Even worse, if he could *do* his Inner Longing's meaning and purpose, Elton was clearly unworthy from all his Past mistakes. They, of course, were his entire fault according to Brother Delegator at Local Gathering. Do do do do do… Any soulish Commoner could see that he didn't have what it took to live an extraordinary Big Dream. He himself was just an ordinary Commoner with ordinary little dreams. Maybe Mediator had meant to give the Big Dream with the books and knife pen to some other Commoner who was more worthy and noble than he? Running rampant in his mind, his delusional thinking consumed him as the passions of his heart grew dimmer and dimmer by each thought.

By now, without the same momentum as before, they crept along, each mile marker harder to pass than the last. Like a deer caught in the headlights, Elton's anxiety grew into an immobilizing fear. He felt paralyzed. Then up ahead he saw a dreadful sign. It read:

YOU ARE NOW LEAVING THE
COMFORT ZONE OF SUBURB OF SOUL.
YOU ARE CROSSING THE BORDER OF DISORDER.
AT YOUR OWN RISK, CAUTIOUSLY PROCEDE OVER
THE ONE-TON BRIDGE ABOVE THE RAGING RIVER.

Now Elton and Elaine both felt sheer terror! Sweat poured down from their foreheads. Like an elephant sitting on their chest, they could hardly breathe. They could hardly think.

Then as they crept closer to the bridge, they were both overcome with an invisible fear they'd never experienced before.

"Our supplies on the trailer along with the weight of the truck and all our baggage is at least Three Tons!" said Elton.

"Yeah. And the journey we planned for demands at least ten more tons of supplies!" Elaine exaggerated with sarcasm.

Elton stopped the truck at the edge of the bridge, unable to advance any further.

Elaine now had tears mixed with the sweat rolling down her face into a puddle in her lap. Elton was perplexed beyond despair. They both sat in the truck with all their sleeping gear piled nice and neat in the bed under the camper shell.

~

After sitting a spell, Elton thought to himself, "Should we turn around, or should we continue the journey together striving to somehow move forward to the unknown in agreement, despite our many differences in the way we'd been thinking, feeling, and acting the past few miles?" This dilemma caused deep pain and confusion for both of them. Letting go of the illusion of control in their soul due to the illusion of light in their flesh was unbearable. Elton was convinced he was making another big mistake.

Time passed.

Then they heard a voice speak these words: "Why have you stopped?"

Elaine recognized Mediators voice first and replied, "I'm scared. I'm not sure I can support Elton adequately with all these fearful feelings consuming me."

"What's the problem, Elaine?" He asked.

"The anger in my partner's eyes and voice are scaring me. And I don't feel safe. How can I feel secure if I can't take all my stuff?" Her soul reacted in emotional terror. "How will Elton provide my needs if we have to leave our baggage and supplies behind? It seems as if he doesn't even want to take care of me anymore. I'd rather take care of my Self. I want to go back to my Perspective Home where I felt safe."

"Are you sure you'd rather live the rest of your life as a second-class citizen of Suburb of Soul—a surviving Commoner knowing you passed up the opportunity of a lifetime?"

"I'm not sure about anything anymore at this point." Elaine mumbled behind her pouty lower lip. "All I know is that I've tried to make this work and give it my best to be the person he wants me to be, but that's not good enough for him."

"No, it's not. And that's not good enough for me, either. You must rely on me to love and respect him *through* you according to who you are *in* me," Mediator spoke matter-of-factly.

Elton, absolutely devastated by the pressure to provide for Elaine when he felt so unappreciated after what she just said, "I'm not, and never have been, the right partner for her in order to pursue our Inner Longings together. This has been a big mistake from the start because I didn't love her with my heart. She deserves better," his soul desperately cried out.

"You *really* mean that '*you*' deserve better… don't you, Elton?" the somber voice spoke directly with a piercing dagger into his flesh. "As long as you *think* with your *emotions*, and conclude that you've made a mistake, believing Elaine is not what you expected, you will never appreciate the gift given to you by me."

"That's not fair," Elton said defensively. "You are the one who put these desires in my heart for a virtuous woman since I was a child. It's according to your Manual For Life, remember? Now I feel stuck with Elaine whom *you* gave me. I've never felt these feelings or acted this way before. I thought I was obeying you, even if I did make a mistake or two in my way of choosing. But this is too much. I'm not the right one for the task at hand."

"Yes, you are," said Mediator promptly. "I chose you for her, and… I chose her for you. Forget about your big ideas and justified arguments you've clung to. You're forfeiting the grace that could be yours by clinging to your worthless idols.

Your memories of the Manual For Life are nothing more than *stale* manna at this point. They have become your master as the letter of the law; but in actuality, you're seeking meaning and purpose for your needs independent of me!—and that is at the root of sin."

"But I don't think I can do this," Elton argued again.

"No, *you* can't. But *I* can. That's what I meant in my Word, *"you can do all things through Mediator."* I need for you to willingly yield your *whole* being to me and exchange the old for the new every day. As the gift Giver, I have provided you with a *good* gift to help you pursue your Big Dream. Be thankful in your thoughts and attitudes with your heart for how I'm finishing the good work I began in you. I know exactly what you need. I created you, remember? I am the author and finisher of your faith and I will also complete what I started as a *good* work inside your heart. Elton, you do not yet understand the things to come. But they're coming. This time will pass and you will have joy and peace like never before. Will you trust me myself to do it?"

"That's what I'm afraid of, the prime time of my youth will pass and I will have lost opportunities to be happy, forever!" Elton anguished over the thought of it. "How can a salt-water fish and a fresh-water fish swim together and be right for each other and happy together?"

"They can't," Mediator said. "But that is not a fair comparison about the value and worth as to how I made you with a new nature—you are not an animal. It's not a matter of how two people are different on the outside. When I breathed spirit-life into your physical body the moment you were conceived in your mother's womb, there came a living soul out of your spirit and body merging together. Where else would your soul have come from? Animals don't have souls. So don't compare yourself to something that doesn't apply. Elton, I have clearly spoken my plan of creation in the Manual For Life. You are a spirit being in a body with a soul. And that, my dear child, is how I created you in my own image. And remember, I desire to have a personal relationship with you. As a new creature in me, I desire to sanctify you through and through; your whole spirit, soul, and body. Elton, you're focusing on the wrong external things due to the fear in your soul. The Fair Exchange begins with the Life Exchanger. He must permeate your whole being from the inside-out. However, unlike your new heart, your feeble thoughts, emotions, and actions will always change like the wind until I give you a new body with a perfect mind. Without understanding the spiritual nature of your heart, you'll never appreciate an unfinished jewel on the outside when you do not value its true worth on the inside."

"So, I guess what you're saying is that it's all my fault. I'm just stuck with Elaine and all my bad decisions in the past until I'm willing to change my attitude."

"Elton," Mediator said, "if you want my favor, revealing the thoughts and attitude of your heart must happen by the Comforter through the dividing power of the written Word. That is why I gave you the Manual For Life. It is living and alive, dividing between soul and spirit... judging the thoughts and attitudes of the heart. Never forget, you must read it fresh everyday as the map leading you to the treasure. But remember also, like due North on a compass, you can only see with the eyes of your heart when there is no wall blocking your vision. Unfortunately, your soulish thoughts—which are different from the thoughts of your spirit—have been conditioned and contaminated by vain philosophies and persuasive arguments according to the traditions of man-made systems. And as for your attitude... well, you're simply lacking gratitude."

~

Elton and Elaine stayed where they were. They watched two unfamiliar fish jump in the river to the right where the water was calm. The distinctly different fish continued to swim along the surface together until they disappeared on the other side. A peculiar looking buck with a black dot on his forehead located just below a magnificent rack of antlers, leaped on the other side of the bridge. Then a doe followed. It was as if to encourage Elton and Elaine to come across. They both knew these were signs but they remained hesitant.

Getting from here to there meant they had to let go of their baggage of fear and take only the necessities by faith—not forfeiting Mediators favor of grace. It seemed way too hard of a task at hand, especially making these decisions together. For a moment, resentment lingered in Elaine and anger filled Elton's soulish thoughts—with justifiable reasons, of course; only legitimate according to the flesh.

After several minutes, they got out of the truck and stood by the bed full of their belongings they clung to for personal meaning and purpose. They looked back fondly toward the skyline of the town where they grew up, remembering all the wonderful comforts—their normal jobs, all their good friends, their Perspective Home, worship at Local Gathering—all part of their comfort zone. As they stood reminiscing, there was actually something special about nothing happening for at least that short simple moment.

Elton and Elaine both got back in the truck. Elton put it in reverse just to see how his soul could once again embrace his thoughts and what Elaine's emotions would feel like again in her flesh.

Oh the thoughts were wonderful at first, and the feelings were spectacular for a split second. Right away, the anxiety went away and they could breath easier.

So Elton revved the engine and engaged the clutch with more gas—just to see what reverse would fulfill.

It was even better and more exhilarating. Going back and ridding their Self of these ridiculous urges in their hearts sounded so good!

They glanced at one another with eager smiles as the truck continued to move faster and faster in reverse—each growing more comfortable. But they suddenly noticed sadness on their faces again. Without hearing the voice, they both knew why. With each moment they traveled back toward town, they were leaving any hope for the Big Dream in their Inner Longings of the heart.

Then, suddenly, they heard Mediator's voice louder than ever, "Why are you going backward?" He demanded.

Elton stopped the truck. "Because I'm afraid leaving Suburb of Soul can just be another mistake on top of all my other mistakes I've been making. Plus, I don't get all this heart and soul stuff. What's the real difference, anyway?"

Elaine spoke up hesitantly, "And... I feel... afraid. I'm scared to leave my familiar family and Perspective Home in Suburb of Soul where my emotions are secure and safe with all the things I've grown accustomed to with my soul. Besides, pursuing our Inner Longings of the heart is too scary and too risky. Neither of us have a clue anymore about the difference between the soul and the heart. We've always been taught that they're the same thing. To me, the thoughts and emotions of soul seem easier to understand."

"Yes, I know it does," Mediator affirmed.

"But if we're *supposed* to pursue our Inner Longings of the heart for more meaning and purpose," Elton proclaimed as matter of fact, "then I'm almost positive from all the empirical evidence I've gathered from my research about human beings, we should *not* feel so afraid if this heart thing is the right thing!"

"On the contrary," Mediator's voice spoke with authority, "yes, you would, just like every soulish Commoner has. It's the fear of losing control that scares you the most. It's the sin nature of your flesh that wants control. That's the reason it's so hard to make the choice in the first place. You must now learn to believe with the faith in your heart... not the soulish thoughts and emotions in your head. Only the noble-minded who eagerly examine the Manual For Life will find the answers their hearts are longing for. But you must hunger and thirst for righteousness... then you will be fulfilled."

Elton and Elaine both sat in disbelief with their heads hung low. They pondered Mediator's words trying to recall if this was accurate according to the Manual For Life from what they'd been taught.

"But you could take away the fear and all the anxiety that comes with it." Elton blurted out.

"Won't you do that for us," Elaine begged. "If you don't, we can't go on!" She added desperately, pleading as if a little girl negotiating with her daddy.

"Yes, you can," Mediator said. "You need to break Free from the Faulty System! Have I not told you in the Manual For Life? *Be strong and courageous. Do not tremble or be terrified. I will be with you wherever you go.* All you need is to meditate with your heart on all the wisdom you've learned from my Word revealed to you by my Comforter. Trust in me with all your heart. Do not rely on your soulish thinking and emotions trying to rationalize spiritual truth for wise decisions. If you foolishly trust in your Self to make choices, you will fail and not be kept safe by spiritual wisdom."

~

Looking back forward in the direction of the unknown, Elton and Elaine discussed their choices. Somewhere out there in the unknown, on the other side of the bridge, held the answers to their Big Dream. They could either keep moving backward toward their comfort zone in Suburb of Soul or forward to the Unknown, in pursuit of the Big Dream in the HeartLand.

"But how am I supposed to be courageous and not get discouraged or terrified if I have all this fear consuming my energy?" Elaine asked Elton.

"Well, I have a boatload of Fear too, but I've been afraid to tell you."

"Why?" Elaine was surprised.

"Because I thought you might not respect me as being strong or trust me to make manly decisions. I've been afraid of people in general not respecting me if they thought I was *weak*."

"Why would I think that? Everyone has fears," Elaine tried to encourage him with reason.

"Because that's what everyone else has ever done in the past."

"You mean all the soulish thinking good-Ole-boy/Old School manly-men in your life, right?"

"Well... I guess so. Maybe. Umm... Yea! You know, you might be on to something. I guess a lot of my fear of rejection is associated more with all the good-OLE-boy/Old School men than it is with women. Wow! I never put that together before. Now that you mention it, I actually thought it was basically *all* Commoners in general, but especially women have been hard on my ego. Sooo... my issues are apparently more directly related to the men, why do you have such a problem with men?"

Elaine, turning two shades of embarrassed-red, hated that the attention shifted on her insecurities. It was only fair that she too allowed her Self to become vulnerable. "Well, I'm going to be honest with you, Elton. Please don't laugh, but I believe most women have Self-esteem issues because of men, especially due to control-freak dads. We women are just as afraid of being seen as weak as what you guys are, just in a different way. When we see our mothers get treated harshly, it destroys our sense of security, emotionally. That's one of the reasons why some of us try so hard to be Daddy's-Girls—we want protection and security from rejection. In fact, that's why it's so hard for us to find a soul-mate who really knows how to care for a woman. Deep down inside, we really *don't* like being a damsel in distress—always week and wimpy needing to be rescued like we see in Disney movies. Those myths from fairytales leave us feeling defeated once the Knight in shining armor conquers the proverbial dragon, gets bored, and moves on to the next adventure—leaving us out of the picture still waiting to be loved.

Emotionally, all those head games feel like rejection, and that only makes us feel powerless, which leads to Self-survival. You see, for us, we become desensitized to our *true* inner beauty believing that's not what you guys really want. All you really want is a hot chick on a motorcycle or sports car to feed your soulish ego! Next, we become demotivated to our Passions of the Heart, which eventually leads to Self-destruction—the bad kind, that is—like eating disorders and cutting. For us women, feeling defeated leads to a hardened heart towards men. It just seems to us all you men really care about is getting something quick and easy to indulge your ego. Sadly, that's become our obsession about our body-image, and that can lead to Self-mutilation." Elaine lowered her head in complete shame for having revealed such a private issue to a guy who will never understand her struggles.

"Wow. I'm really sorry about that," Elton said with deep remorse. "No one's ever explained that to me before how women have those kind of feelings and how that effects your value and worth. I guess my mother and sisters held all those emotions inside because my dad acted like he didn't really care. But in a lot of ways, I think we men really *can* relate more than we're willing to admit. I know for me, you and I can relate to each other's thoughts and feelings more than I ever realized before. You know, now that I think about it, it's probably not a gender thing—it's a human thing. Wow, maybe there really is a difference between our heart and our soul that makes us similar? But can I tell you something really personal? I still have a big fear. I really do worry deep inside about you thinking of me as weak and insecure. That's why it's been so hard to be open and vulnerable with my heart at times when I feel that way. As a man, I need validation and affirmation through respect. I don't know if you know this, but guys need validation, especially from their fathers. But when we don't get it, I guess we turn to our mothers, sisters, girlfriends, and wives—and eventually it's easier to turn to quick fixes like pornography. I've never admitted this to anyone else but Common Sense. I did go to a Pselfologist. He just prescribed a pill and told me I had a problem with anxiety. He said I should try changing the way I think, feel and act toward my Self around others. None of that helped. It made me feel like it was somehow all my fault why I had issues. That's why I finally took your advice and called Common Sense. Despite his background in Pselfology, he always begins with the inside-out approach."

"Wow, Elton," Elaine said with compassion, "your openness like this only makes me love and respect you more. I just wish you wouldn't wait so long to come to this place. When you're willing to be vulnerable with me, I melt inside. Honestly? …it becomes your most attractive quality. I've seen how hard it is for you as a guy to let that tender side of your heart be seen — let alone trust me with it. To me, that's the part I want to connect with for the rest of our lives together."

~

Elton decided if the presence of fear wasn't going away, he would simply have to man-up and put the truck back in forward gear.

Knowing that their tremblings inside were still an issue, they reached out and held each other's hand. They were in this journey together and stronger for it. Elaine felt safe again, so she scooted back over next to Elton as they conjured up the courage from their hearts to move forward in the direction of the unknown.

But they both knew they had to let go of the extra baggage in the back of the truck and unhitch the trailer with extra supplies in order to get across the one-ton rickety old bridge. Otherwise, their extra weight would collapse the bridge and they'd plunge down into the Raging River.

Even though their fear remained ever present, they clung to the words of Mediator as they relied upon faith and each other to move forward across the bridge. They passed the sign again, but this time they ignored its message as they broke through the invisible barrier of Fear.

It was at that moment that Elton and Elaine made an amazing discovery.

Looking back beyond the sign stood a mound of supplies and baggage they didn't think or feel they could do without. They broke free of their comfort zone. Overcoming the illusion of light associated with their old values and beliefs, Elton also learned to let go of the good-Ole-boy/Old Schooler mentality.

Consequently, the wall from fear was no longer surrounding the passions of their hearts. They were free to move forward on their journey pursuing the HeartLand with confidence and courage.

They began to sing their song again, driving with a much lighter load without fear distracting them. Only this time, they were about to find out another hard lesson due to their choice.

Hungry and a little bit tired, they stopped to have a picnic. After they ate, both Elaine and Elton took out their Journey Journals and wrote with their knife-pens about all the things that happened so far that day and the new truths they learned about overcoming fears.

It's a very good thing they did, because they were about to face something neither could have anticipated.

Chapter 5 Journey Journal

Our next step can be the most critical so far for most. Elton, along with Elaine, had to learn a big lesson why it's so important that believers must experience Brokenness before experiencing Wholeness. Like them, we must learn to yield our Self to Mediator in the Spirit (1st Cor. 6:17). Now we are going to consider how the process produces Fruitfulness when we overcome footholds and strongholds (Gal. 5:22-24). What we mean by "spiritual brokenness" is anything due to Self-control issues where there's an idol we're clinging to keeping us from discovering we *can't* <u>do</u> it ourselves. Instead, we need to become dependent on God, so Mediator will live through us (Jonah 2:8).

Consequently, footholds & strongholds are anything and anyone contradicting the fruit of the Spirit resulting in habitual, addictive behaviors leading to disobedience due to disbelief. Our painful disappointments/traumas often result in <u>F</u>rustration, <u>R</u>esentment, <u>A</u>nger, and <u>B</u>itterness, which leaves us sick from unresolved issues unable to "forgive" or be "thankful." (Emphasis is on unforgiveness). Therefore, Footholds & Strongholds depend on what <u>you're</u> "Holding" on to:

- **Are you holding on to your <u>past</u> "successes" and accomplishments**, producing bad fruit of pride and Self-righteousness continuing to tempt you to be Self-reliant. (Phil. 3:9) Yes or No Please explain your answer.

———————————————————————————————

———————————————————————————————

———————————————————————————————

———————————————————————————————

- **Are you holding on to your <u>past</u> "hurts"** from being manipulated through abusive fear, shame, guilt and pain leading to rejection—manifesting bad fruit in two major ways: disapproval and abandonment? Yes or No Please explain your answer.

_____

_____

_____

_____

- **Are you holding on to your <u>past</u> "rights"** when entitlement causes bad fruit like: *"why don't I have rights, why do I have to surrender what is mine to keep?"* Yes or No Please explain your answer.

_____

_____

_____

_____

- **Are you holding on to your <u>present</u> "resistance"** to being spiritually broken? Yes or No Please explain your answer.

_____

_____

_____

_____

Remember, don't live out of thoughts and feelings, because they can be equally deceptive to the decision making process. When it comes to head-knowledge vs. experiential-knowing, the way our thoughts and emotions deal with truth is not enough to keep us free because the effect of sin on our mind is *greater* than a book knowledge understanding of truth, i.e., possessing knowledge from Bible studies while indulging the flesh... sin *prevails*. But active experiential-knowing in the Spirit is what keeps us safe and makes us free from sins power. It is only when we walk in spiritual wisdom (1st Cor. 2) that we are kept safe from sin's destructive power over our good intentions. Even though we intend to live free from sin's *control*, we are not free from its *influence* or *effect* unless we put to death daily the flesh. Although the flesh is weak, that's why "Free indeed" actually means "free to *choose*". But we are *not obligated* to sin, neither are thoughts and emotions a sin. *"He who trusts in himself (psyche - thoughts & emotions) is a fool, but he who walks in wisdom is kept safe."* (Prov. 28:26)

From an outside-in perspective, our life experiences and circumstances might tell us different, because according to worldly philosophy, there are two kinds of people: those who have been rejected, and those who are being rejected. However, even though we will be rejected by people; God's acceptance is always *enough*, right? Answer these next critical questions:

When abandoned by others, why does it sometimes feel like God's presence and acceptance are not enough?

_____

_____

_____

_____

If we are disapproved of, why do we sometimes think God's approval and acceptance are not enough?

_____

_____

_____

_____

If we are mistreated harshly by others, why do we sometimes consider the lie that God's love and acceptance are not enough?

_____

_____

_____

_____

If we fail and screw up, why do we sometimes throw in the towel and start acting as though God's grace and acceptance are not enough?

_____

_____

_____

_____

If we lose all of our material possessions, why do we sometimes feel sorry for our Self and consider God's provisions and acceptance are not enough?

_____

_____

_____

_____

3 lies (footholds & strongholds) we accept in the flesh by our thoughts, feelings, and actions:

1. **The *thought-lies:* What I dwell on impacts the way I think about myself.**

    Example – "I think God withholds His Big Dream from someone like me because I'm at fault."

Example – "I think God is too high and lofty for me, thus, because he's a Holy God... I don't measure up."

Example – "I think God loves special people by grace who mess up in their flesh – therefore, some who sin are OK."

Interpretation: "I think these thoughts therefore I do not trust myself, God, or others; thus, I have a difficult time relating and having fellowship with the Lord and others."

2. **The *feeling-lies:* What I express emotionally impacts the way I feel about myself.**

Example – "I feel I'm *not* acceptable, lovable, good enough, normal!"

Example – "I feel I'm smart and successful in my own strength – I don't need help like the less fortunate."

Example – "I feel when something bad happens to me, it is God's punishment."

Interpretation: "I'm suffering from feelings of insecurity and inadequacy. Therefore, I can't trust myself not to compromise. I either settle for less; think too highly of myself with feelings of superiority remaining Self-righteous as a smokescreen; or look for love in wrong places because I deserve less than the best."

3. **The *action-lies:* What I do in my behavior impacts how I treat myself.**

Example – "The way I act around other people (parents, spouse, friends) is who I am."

Example – "The way people treat me is probably a reflection of what I deserve."

Example – "The way my circumstances don't work out probably reflects my poor choices."

Interpretation: "I do not trust others (even myself) to have my best interest in mind; I've become fearful and suspicious, Self protective with a wall; hurt, angry, shut down, assume the worst in situations. Always having a backdoor to avoid and escape."

Most of us, when we struggle with footholds and strongholds, try to overcome these temptations by saying things like, "I am a believer... I shouldn't be tempted like this..." That method will always lead to defeat. Why? Because it is putting "law" on yourself causing you to depend on your effort to work it out rather than by the Spirit. Oddly enough, sin actually uses "law" as a means of control to gain power in the flesh (Romans 7:4). God's way of overcoming temptation is to begin realizing that temptation is not sin. Even Mediator was tempted but He did not sin. When tempted, take yourself out from under the law in your mind and obey Mediator even when you don't see immediate results. However, remember that a purpose without a plan is just good intentions. It is wise to have a purpose with a plan that goes something like this:

S W O T - S P O T

Maximize – **Strengths (empowering Inner Longings for the Meaning of the Journey)**

Minimize – **Weaknesses (overcoming vulnerabilities of past thoughts and feelings)**

Optimize – **Opportunities (maintaining single focus on the Purpose at hand)**

Ostracize – Threats (Keeping every thought captive to avoid oppositions)

Strategize – Solutions (personalize opportunities and be prepared for other options)

Prioritize – Problems (disregard distractions by asking the right questions, first!)

Organize – Options (itemize practical choices from available recourses)

Theorize – Thoughts (discover new ideas from a new perspective)

And finally, we need a helpful Fruit Inspection Check-List that will help keep things in perspective.

Fruit Inspection Check-List

Fear-Lies That Spoil Fruit.	Freedom-Truths That Produce Fruit
I need to do something to be someone.	I need to be someone to do something.
I need to be strong to live for God.	I am week but Christ makes me strong.
I need to learn how to cope.	I need to turn to God for hope.
I need a program to walk in the light.	I need a person who is the light.
I need a list to follow procedures.	I need the Lord to finish good measures.
I need behavioral modification.	I need identity clarification.
I need to hold on to what I have.	I need to let go in the direction of God.
I need to achieve victory the best I can.	I need to receive VICTORY by God's plan.
I need a new prescription for symptoms.	I need a new perspective for problems.

Jesus said, "You will know the truth and the truth will make you free."(John 8:32).

Chapter 6

The Crazy Makers

Later that evening, not far from the sign, Elton and Elaine got back into the truck and once again headed toward the Border of Disorder. Just before the bridge, Elton and Elaine's journey came to a screeching halt. As the road sloped downward, just ahead to the left they saw a breathtaking view of churning white water. At the Y, two rivers merged with force and determination creating a deep gorge from all the turbulence. As beautiful and wondrous as one can imagine, the thunderous roar made for a spectacular, yet terrifying scene as the two Seekers noticed how rickety and narrow the bridge appeared over the Raging River.

Elaine was first to be surprised what she noticed next walking in the middle of the road near the bridge—a lot of Commoners from Suburb of Soul. There was one, looking very familiar, hurrying toward her.

It was her mother, Embellisher.

Hoping she would escape an embarrassing moment, Elaine got out of the truck acting as if she was checking something in the back. Like a seen right out of Gone With The Wind in a Scarlet O'Hare drama-queen moment, Embellisher hurried faster and faster then threw her arms around her, "Oh, Sweet Pea!" she cried. "My little girl is safe! I'm so thankful. I came just in the nick of time to save you from this big horrible mistake. I know this must be so hard on you marrying such a foolish young man who doesn't know how to take care of you properly. I feel as if I did something wrong and failed you somehow. Do you blame me at all?"

"Oh Momma, stop all your drama, please. It's getting old and I'm not falling for that anymore. I'm not going to let you push my guilt buttons or shame me and Elton for the sake of your feelings. It's not all about you and your poor little pity parties. Goodness! I'm so tired of worrying about how my decisions will impact your life. Please, get a grip on reality. And how in the world did you get here so quickly?" Elaine asked after a barrage of normally unspoken frustration. She was usually the compliant daughter who'd massage all those emotions full of guilt and shame, enabling her mom's unhealthy feelings festering if she wasn't soothed by some feel-sorry-for-her attention.

"Oh, daughter of mine, don't you dare speak to me in that tone of voice!" Embellisher was taken back. "For your information, when Commoners aren't actually *leaving* Suburb of Soul, you don't have to worry about all the baggage and supplies to carry. I got here in lickety split!"

"But mom, why are you here and in such a hurry? You seemed fine with my decision when we talked on the phone."

"Well, young lady, I know that you told us you were going, but I never thought you would actually go through with it. I insist, you must not go through with this crazy notion. Me and the whole family were beyond ourselves when your sister told us that you and Elton were *really* serious. That's never been like you to be so irresponsible. Sweetie, everyone knows Commoner's get a whim now and then, and even a *nagging urge* at least once in their lifetime. But no one really goes through with it… well, at least no one in their right mind, that is." as she looked straight at Elton with her cutting eyes. "Honestly, what were the two of you thinking, especially you Elton. This is not safe. I trusted you with my precious daughter's well-being. She could get hurt. She could even die! Just look at that rickety old bridge! And then there's the unknown through the Forbidden Forest."

"But we share a Big Dream together, mother!" Elaine finally got the courage to stand up and defended her husband. "It's *my* decision too. Don't accuse Elton and attack his motives. I trust him and we're in this together. This is our Inner Longings for more meaning and purpose and we want to pursue it without having to worry about you."

She tried to confront her Mother with her big greenish-brown eyes staring without a blink. Yet, attempting to reassure her that they unloaded their extra baggage and supplies. But the sight of the rickety bridge over the Raging River disturbed Embellisher even more as she cringed at the sight of the turbulent waters below.

~

Elton's father, Control Freak, approached next. "I was wondering when you'd do something stupid like this to me. So, Big Dreamer, you've gone ahead with your plans to fulfill your Big Dream after all—as if your God's gift to this world!" he spoke with a harsh critical tone. "Hey knuckle-head, did you forget that your Scotts-Irish family comes from a long line of hardy good-Ole-boy Commoners. Doesn't that mean anything to you? We Old-Schoolers have our pride in our stoic roots. And I'm proud to say, up until now, not one has ventured off to pursue these crazy notions for a Big Dream. Do you think you're the only one whose gotten rocked in your sleep? Son, do you realize you're going completely against our good-Ole-boy traditions? You're too smart for this sort of thing, Elton. I raised you better than this. I bet your emotional wife talked you into this, didn't she? Grow up and be a man! Don't let a woman tell you what to do. That's not macho. Take charge! Don't be a sissy... letting a woman manipulate you with her silly emotions. And another thing, why should the two of you become Seekers when the rest of us have always been content conforming to what's always been done according to the performance-based system?"

Before Elton could defend his wife or respond with his heart, Brother Delegator offered a piece of advice. "Elton, along with your father, I've always had high hopes for you."

"My father? You know as well as I do my father never had high hopes for me!" Elton rebuttaled quickly. "Who are you fooling now? I don't trust you anymore to represent Mediator as a good shepherd, let alone care for what's in my personal best interest. Forget about me. Just look at Elaine. How can you stand there and not protect those under your care getting slammed with all these manipulative tactics?" Elton was now in a state of anger about ready to explode.

"Actually," Brother Delegator looked around to make sure everyone was listening, "I overheard Embellisher mention how we've all experienced wacky dreams and crazy notions a time or two, isn't that right everyone?" The whole crowd shouted A-men like a Choir in agreement. "But those are just fantasies. It's not real. And don't believe all that hogwash about the difference between soul and spirit. That's an inaccurate interpretation of the Manual For Life. Take it from someone who's studied the languages and been to seminary. The term 'heart' is just what we use for Soul and Spirit interchangeably. There's no real difference according to all my formal training and studies. Come on, get with the program and back to your senses about how to think and feel with your soul. That's what we all do in Suburb of Soul. Let me ask you again, you don't really want to leave all that stuff you've accomplished and acquired behind, do you?. Get over your Self. Think of others. Look at your family. They need you. I need you! Don't be so Selfish!" It was almost as if Brother Delegator memorized these lines as a script and sounding like a broken record. "One last thing, Elton, I've backed you up through a lot of bad decisions before, but I can't support you making the biggest mistake of your life."

Both Elton and Elaine were speechless, overcome with shame and guilt. They'd heard about Crazy-Makers at the Border of Disorder before, but never suspected they existed like this. Crazy-Makers were supposed to be strangers with a grudge, but for sure no one they knew personally. They never imagined in their wildest dreams Crazy-Makers could be some of their closest relatives, friends, and acquaintances.

Now, along with all the others, Elaine's mother and sister, Elton's father, and Brother Delegator all stood their ground in front of the Bridge keeping these Seekers from pursuing their Big Dream.

What was going to happen? Were Elaine and Elton going to stick together or become separated due to these unhealthy affections for these family and friends? They needed a moment to think about the situation and figure out what they were feeling in the midst of their dilemma.

They asked their Crazy-Makers to give them some time to talk things over. They took a walk over to the edge of the high bank overlooking the turbulent waters, where they sat down on a smooth rock holding each other in their arms. Confusion and bewilderment consumed their soul. Trying to block out the thunderous roar of the water, Elton thought about Elaine and what she must be feeling. Like those two rivers merging into one, they both felt their lives were on a collision course. Overwhelmingly, they began to wonder if maybe their Crazy-Makers might be right. Maybe *they* were the one's wrong to go through with pursuing *their* Big Dream together.

~

Then they heard what sounded like footsteps crunching gravel. When they turned to the left to see who it was, they were pleasantly surprised their good friend, Common Sense, was approaching.

"Common Sense!" Elton belted out. "Are we ever glad to see you. What amazing timing you have? We were sitting here pondering whether or not to cross the bridge to pursue our Big Dream."

Common Sense pulled up a rock and joined them in the midst of their stupor. "When I heard the rumor going around town that you both decided to leave today for the HeartLand, I just had to come and see if it was true," he reassured them of his support. "Plus, I know from experience that you can't get past these Crazy-Makers on your own and keep your sanity!"

They all laughed.

"We can't thank you enough," Elaine sweetly replied. "But do you see how many there are and *who* they are?"

"Oh yeah, I see them alright. I saw a bunch of commotion headed out of town and knew I had to get here quickly. They're Crazy-Makers, all right. I had the exact same thing happen to me. My family and friends thought I was absolutely nuts, so they thought they'd do me a favor and rescue me from my Self."

"What did you do?" Elton asked.

"I'm about to show you. But remember one thing, it's not what you do, it's about a wiser approach according to who you are. Remember, you have to trust me. You see, for this particular situation, just think of me as your Crazy-Maker rescuer. I'm here to help you overcome the resistance of their opposition."

Then Common Sense explained exactly what was happening. "Elaine, your mother and sister are in cahoots with each other using guilt trip tactics. They obviously think your too naïve and weak. And Elton, your father and Brother Delegator are using mental manipulation to sabotage your efforts. They obviously think you're out of touch with your right mind. However, here's the kicker, even though these are very important *personal* relationships, please try to understand when I say *don't* take it personally. They're actually *doing* what comes naturally from a soulish perspective. When you left your comfort zone, you didn't mean to, but you affected theirs dramatically. Each of them has to face their own fears of something or someone they've lost in their past if you move forward with your future."

"That really makes a lot of sense when you think about it," Elton added. "But what do I do now? How do I get all our Crazy-Makers to see what we are doing is what's *best* for us?"

"Well, you might be able to help them see the truth if you quit focusing on the *doing* so much and simply *be* who you really are based on who you were always meant to become! The presence of the Comforter is the key to leverage. One thing for sure... don't try to match wits, because that's the strategy of the soul. Being different in your new nature must make the difference in who you are with your heart. But you can only make a difference if you really are different. They must see that you have a peace with a solid foundation standing on the Manual For Life. They must become convinced beyond a shadow of a doubt that you are *certain* of your convictions about the heart—that's what faith's all about. Otherwise, they will play on your thoughts and emotions in your soul... even if they have to resort to sabotage. They will drive you insane by creating a wedge between the two of you."

"If we can't find common ground, then why try to reason with them at all!" Elaine cried in despair.

"Try to establish an understanding of their *values*," Common Sense continued, "that will help you figure out what's motivating *them*. Seek to learn the intent behind their concerns. This is one of the most important times to be quick to listen and slow to speak and ask questions before coming to any conclusions. I know that some Crazy-Makers operate in foolishness, try to avoid them and simply dismiss their actions... even if it comes from a family member. Trust me, it's not worth the time or energy. But most Crazy-Makers have genuine concerns that make sense to their soul... they just have bad methods because they are acting out of desperation, which is the fear of loss—not the Inspiration for gain. They can only see what they're losing instead of what you are gaining. So it's up to you to inspire them out of a win-win situation. Believe it or not, they are the ones who can actually help you bring clarity to the plans of your own destination. That's how Seekers no longer conform to the old by turning opposition into opportunity."

As Common Sense positioned his footing to leave, he said, "Cling to your Inner Longings for all you're worth. Elton and Elaine, you're both destined for the Fair Exchange, I just know it!"

They all embraced each other in a group hug, and as their good friend left the scene, his last words were, "Remember, when Crazy-Makers try to block you from crossing over the Bridge, what matters most is who you choose to *be* no matter the cost!"

~

As Elton and Elaine pondered those final words, they knew all too well it was time to speak with their Crazy-Makers.

In the setting evening sun, together they spoke with each one individually to show their united strength as well as their openness to every concern. Elaine was much better at asking questions and encouraging the Crazy-Makers to give *them* a listening ear when it was their turn to share. As they walked back and forth near the water's edge, they shared openly with each one about their recent experience hearing from Mediator about their Big Dream—as well as what they discovered about their own unique Inner Longings of the heart. They took the time to learn from all the various concerns and found out the real intent behind each one's motives connected to their values.

"Wow! What a difference this approach truly makes," Elton thought to his Self. They got better results than they could ever have expected with the help from Common Sense. Then they told everyone they made their final decision to pursue their Big Dream in the HeartLand with or without their support.

By sundown, Elton and Elaine were ready to cross over the Bridge. As most of the Crazy-Makers had a change of attitude and gave their blessings, there was not a dry eye among them… well, there was just one.

"I've changed my opinion," Brother Delegator told Elton, "you're not being Selfish after all. You have my total support to pursue your Big Dream. In fact, I'm going to tell all your good friends back at Local Gathering to support you too. I think we all wish we had the courage you and Elaine have together to come out of our comfort zone and take a risk to pursue our own Big Dreams. Be sure and let me know how everything works out." They hugged good-bye.

Elaine's mother and sister walked her to the truck. "You know Sweet Pea; I spoke with your Father on the phone and told him what you and Elton are doing. He actually told me to tell you he supports you. At first I thought he was crazy. But, I think he feels really bad he let his own opportunity slip away years ago. I'm ashamed to admit it, but I'm to blame for that. Our passions almost gave into crazy notions after you were born. He wanted to take the risk together, but foolishly, I was too afraid, and that's what destroyed our marriage. I think your father still resents me but respects you and Elton for having the courage to *be* rather than always to *do*. Please understand, that's all I've ever known from my parents and their parents. I just haven't always understood you the way you needed me to. But I feel as if you've helped me to understand something deeper inside my own heart than ever before." With tears in their eyes, her mother and sister quietly walked toward the side of the bridge.

With final waves and blowing kisses, Elton started the truck, revved the engine, and headed toward the bridge.

~

In the fading daylight of dusk's colorful delight, Elton and Elaine saw the silhouette of a man standing in the middle of the bridge. At first, Elton recoiled from the thought this might be his father, who never gave his blessing or said good-bye. But the Commoner who stood in the middle of the Bridge was far more threatening to them. This Commoner was not just any soulish Commoner—he was the governor of Suburb of Soul. Dictator governed with an iron fist according to his performance-based standard. He was the one who decided the terms for values and beliefs of the soul and determined what was right for Commoners. He owned every shop in town. He even owned the bridge. Heck, he owned most Local Gatherings.

"Stop!" he said, "I am not inclined to give you my permission to cross my bridge."

"With all due respect, sir," Elton politely said, "why will you not give us permission?"

"Because you are a Commoner and I need you to remain in Suburb of Soul where it is all *good*. Besides, these are crazy notions you are entertaining. Notions that are leading you on the road to the unknown for something you think you will find somewhere, and someday at *best*. Nonsense! Turn around and go back to your normal Perspective Home and we'll all forget this ever happened."

"But, what if we promise to return?" Elaine pleaded.

"Hogwash! You can't make me that promise and keep it. Eventually, your new Self will think you are better than the rest of us. You will put your new perspective on a pedestal looking down at those you feel you're better than."

"We would never do that!" Elaine barked back, offended at the notion. "We received a Big Dream from Mediator who has also shown us signs that we *are* Seekers already. In fact, we will one day experience the Fair Exchange together and come back and share it with everyone. Why wouldn't you want the "*best*" for everyone, anyway?"

"Nothing but dreamers and go-getters is what you *really* are. I believe Mediator only helps those who help their Self. That's how I turned things around for this town."

"No, that's not true. You're lying!" Elton said matter-of-factly. "The Manual For Life says just the opposite of what you've brainwashed every Commoner to believe. But know this, according to the Manual For Life, I've been heartwashed. And your mistaken quotations mean nothing to me anymore. According to the Manual For Life, the one and only Mediator lovingly helps those who realize they're helpless apart from Him. We're all helpless to accomplish anything of eternal worth in our own strength. That's why we'll *always* need Mediator, not some imposter like you."

At this very despairing moment, Elaine tried hard not to give in to a panic attack, and Elton tried hard not to have a mental meltdown. The better part of wisdom from their hearts told them they should not argue with a fool—the worse kind of Crazy-Maker. They realized—more than ever before—Dictator had invested a lot of time and money into each Commoner with an unfair exchange. He had a lot of power and control to lose, and he wasn't about to let go without a fight.

What should they do? What *could* they do? Then they remembered Common Sense's last words to *be* not to *do* …no matter the cost.

And so they decided it was worth abandoning their truck and all their stuff, with only one essential bag to take with them, to simply swim across the Raging River on the calm side to the right of the bridge.

That's when they decided to take a swim.

Of course, with the undertow, there was still a possibility they wouldn't make it. The deep and wide waters were very intimidating, and only Elaine was a strong swimmer. But they knew they had to at least give it a try… no matter the cost!

As everyone looked on, Elton helped Elaine down to the waters edge where the surface was calm. Despite the fear of swirling undercurrents in the middle, they were both about to dive in when all of a sudden something grabbed their attention nearby. It was something they couldn't see from above. Just around the river bend, there was a wide opening to a cave-like tunnel leading beneath the Raging River coming out the other side.

"We don't have to cross the bridge after all!" Elton shouted with hilarity. "No wonder why Dictator put up all those signs about the bridge. They were only distractions so we wouldn't see the tunnel."

When they got back in their truck, they found a note on the steering wheel. Elton read it out loud to Elaine:

Elton and Elaine, if you find this letter then you found the tunnel, and now I know you'll choose to obey Mediator and leave your extra baggage and supplies behind. This is a Faith Journey, and you must completely depend on Him to be your Great Provider from here on out. Enjoy a dry path through Raging River. Your Big Dreams are waiting for you on the other side in the HeartLand! You've got my word. — Common Sense

Elton and Elaine were filled with peace as they drove the truck through the tunnel.

As they proceeded with the windows down, all the cheers grew less and less. Soon they were on their own again, making it to the other side. Once they knew for sure Suburb of Soul was finally behind them, they waved one last time for old time sake.

However, it was now too dark to tell if anyone saw them or even the red tail-lights glowing in the darkness.

Later that night... before they stopped to sleep, Elton and Elaine discussed what they would write in their Journey Journals in addition to what they had written earlier that same day.

They needed a good night of sleep in order to be alert the next day finding the secretive entrance into the Forbidden Forest.

Chapter 6 Journey Journal

As followers of Mediator—now Seekers—Elton and Elaine were surprised about the Crazy-Makers, especially who they were. We too have Crazy-Makers. Only, we usually don't suspect them to be family, friends, or close associates. But they often are. They too get caught up in the faulty system, almost as victims of circumstances.

Ok... so who are some of your Crazy-Makers?

_____

_____

_____

_____

Consequently, often times we ourselves listen to misquotes from those whom we've trusted to look out for us, especially when seeking comfort during difficult times. We don't expect to be blindsided. After all, people of faith (Commoners) make it their goal to believe with their soul according to the good book, right? Excuse the sarcasm, but aren't we a little naïve—in a world full of performance— trusting some of those closest to us? Do we detect our misguided caregivers por- trayal or semblance of the truth when it comes to matters of the heart? Since my own personal quest has led me to be more determined than ever by asking 'why do I believe what I say I believe?' my studies have proven over and over how things were often taken completely out of context (i.e. Joel 2:25, *"Then I will make up to you for the years that the swarming locust has eaten, The creeping locust, the stripping locust and the gnawing locust...*, and then I read the entire rest of the verse?... *My great army which I sent among you."*) What! Mediator sent the locust? These terrible hideous creatures in all the stages of destruction! Now that just can't be right. Surely that's a misprint. My great Mediator could not possibly be the one who wreaks such havoc in the life of a believer, could He? Heck, if that's the case, who needs the enemy?

Ok... be honest. What are some misquotes you've recognized that came straight from your Crazy-Makers?

_____

_____

_____

_____

As disillusioning as this may seem, Mediator is for us... and often times because we are our own worst enemy, He must take us out of our comfort zone with force. He will even allow those around to make things worse.

How many times have you felt fear and disappointment due to the sabotage of others, feeling as though you were set up for failure?

_____

_____

_____

_____

Probably the most difficult disappointment of all is when we feel as though Mediator has let us down. Unfortunately, our faithfulness does not always line up with His purpose and plan. There are times He makes things difficult so we will turn loose of those things and relationships we are desperately holding on to. As a matter of fact, listen to the words of Mediator in Matt. 10:34 - *"Do not think that I came to bring peace on the earth; I did not come to bring peace, but a sword;"* For most of us, we got the distinct impression He came to bring peace on earth, at least, that's what we're told at Christmas time, right?

Are you experiencing difficulties among those closest to you through sadness, anguish, anger, or anxiety?

Yes   or   No   Explain why you believe God just might be allowing that condition to get your attention!

_____

_____

_____

_____

Oswald Chamber put it like this in his daily devotional, <u>My Utmost For His Highest</u>: *"Watch for all you are worth until you hear the Bridegroom's voice in the life of another. Never mind what havoc it brings, what upsets, what crumblings of health; rejoice with divine hilarity when once His voice is heard. You may often see Jesus Christ wreck a life before He saves it."* Even though Mediator, our heavenly bridegroom, oftentimes determines extreme levels of personal heartaches (including forsaking loved ones, losing health–property–possessions-finances-careers-accomplishments and even social status, etc. Matt. 4:18-22; 10:24-42; Luke 5:27-28; 9:57-62; 14:25-27; 18:28-30), be careful not to allow your circumstances scare you into believing you're all alone. Remember, Jesus promised by the power and presence of His Spirit He would be with you always throughout the duration of your journey hear on earth.

In what ways are you able to depend on Mediator even when almost everyone else seems to let you down?

_____

_____

_____

_____

We all could use a good friend like Common Sense. His practical advice is the cure we can use in the midst of despair and confusion. Often times we get defensive when facing opposition, especially when those we thought we could trust to cover our back are the ones who carry the biggest knives stabbing us in the back. However, it is certainly true that "Values" are the greatest determining factor when it comes to motives and intent. In fact, in the final analysis, researches have proven that "Values" are #1 issue determining a persons choice for a better quality of life. Instead of an emotional reaction, we must submit to a wise response. One of the greatest solutions for better results during conflict resolution: ASK QUESTIONS FIRST BEFORE COMING TO ANY CONCLUSIONS!

Here are a few good questions with a practical approach when needing to defuse the anger of others driving us in sane.

? **Question:** I believe in who you are deep inside your heart, and I hope you trust me when I say I don't want to make a mistake in my decision. That's why I really want to know why you believe I'm making a bad choice from your perspective?

? **Question:** I'm hoping you wouldn't take the time and come out of your way to talk with me unless you really do care about what's in my best interest. So, I appreciate your concern and need to know what it is that you believe I might be missing?

? **Question:** From your perspective, what is it that you are concerned about with me the most?

? **Question:** We may not always see eye to eye, but I really care about your opinion. Please forgive me if I don't always take your advice, but I'm hoping you respect me enough as someone who takes the initiative to seek ways in which to improve my life, even if it's taking a risk. Can I count on your support even if I make a mistake?

Write down some practical ways you can "be" to live out of your identity in front of others in response to these following statements!

Be willing to humbly evaluate your weaknesses first (Matthew 5:29)

Make no provision for the flesh in response to others - (Romans 13:14; Romans 6:13)

Walk by the Spirit and test the spirit of others - (Galatians 5:16, 1 John 4:1)

Deal with the distorted views of others by replacing them with truth according to the Bible (Acts 17:11)

Ask Mediator to live His life though you daily – (Galatians 2:20; Phil 1:21; Romans 15:18)

Chapter 7

Finding the Path
Through the Forbidden Forest

⌐‿⌐

A fter sleeping soundly under the camper shell that night, Elaine and Elton woke to a bright, beautiful sun-shiny day. The fear of leaving their Comfort zone along with all the Crazy-Makers was behind them now… well, at least they wanted to believe.

Dictator, on the other hand, was relentless. Lurking not far in the distance, he was not one to give up that easily, especially knowing they still had to find the hidden passage through the Forbidden Forest. He had a few more tricks up his sleeve to sabotage these young dreamers from achieving their Big Dream. He also knew that when influential Commoner's like Elton and Elaine succeed fulfilling their Inner Longings, it only encouraged others to have hope getting off the performance-based treadmill and following the same journey. So, he had to try and steal, kill and destroy all hope of them ever reaching the HeartLand if he was to keep his control over Suburb of Soul.

The truck started up without a hitch, and their ability to move forward came with the greatest of ease as they traveled toward the unknown without their trailer. Out of consideration for his young bride, and before they passed Raging River through the tunnel, Elton had asked Common Sense to put his trailer with Elaine's stuff back in their garage at their Perspective Home, ...and so he did.

Around each and every turn, they expected to see the next sign that Common Sense had told them about. This was an unspoken and unseen sign no one could hear or see on the outside. If they could see it or hear it with their external senses of their soul, then so could Dictator, who had never been able to find it.

But they didn't think it or feel it, either. Instead, they drove half the day through bends and steep slopes. They soon found themselves at a wide cross-road where every direction looked the same, but there was not a path to be found. With map and compass in hand, Elaine became Elton's co-pilot/navigator feeling pretty good about this navigating stuff. She had helped him up to this point, but nothing felt right about the next choice to make.

So Elton stopped to get some gas at a strange little station with a large unattractive building in the back. One pump. One nozzle. And only a one-man stall with one small window for paying. As he pulled out his wallet, there was a sign that read, No Checks or Credit Cards from Suburb of Soul. Cash Only! Stricken with fear, Elton had only withdrawn a small amount of cash before they left. He knew their funds were limited, but they had deposited plenty of money in the bank back at Suburb of Soul to last them a while.

He paid the clerk whom he could not see. Then he asked, "Would you by any small chance know which direction is the HeartLand?"

A scuffle, a high-pitched feedback, then a screeching whisper came through the small speaker, "You might speak a little more quietly of these things around here. I would advise you to take your truck through the washer in the back and get cleaned up before you continue your journey."

"But... I don't need a car wash. My truck is fine," Elton said with confidence.

"No, you ninny. Your truck is not clean enough for the rest of your travels if you are to find what you are looking for. Go now and do not say another word!"

With great hesitation, Elton drove his clean white truck around to the back where he did find a car wash. Stranger things could *not* have happened at this point—confusing Elaine's sense of direction.

"What are we doing?" she asked. "Why are we going through a car wash when our truck is perfectly clean?"

"I don't know," Elton replied. "The clerk inside that small booth said this is what we needed to do when I asked him for directions."

After a large barn-looking door opened from behind a wall blocking any view from the road, a flashing green sign encouraged them to move forward. Once the left front wheel was on the track, Elton put the truck into neutral as the conveyer grabbed the front tires and pulled them inside. All the normal noises of squirting sprayers and clothy brushes began to wash their already clean truck. The fresh smell of greenish detergents along with a waxy finish seemed like the washer they'd always gone to near their Perspective Home in Suburb of Soul. As the windy blowers completed the process, they both noticed things weren't the same outside—especially the new forest-green color camouflaging their truck. Nothing but thick brush and tall trees were all around them with a fairly wide country road in front of them.

"That's it!" Elaine yelled with excitement. "That's the path through the Forbidden Forest."

A green light came on with the words, ENTERING THE UNKNOWN WILDERNESS.

The driving was easier and their gas gauge barely moved as they traveled into the Unknown Wilderness. Around each bend, they expected to see the HeartLand. But again, they didn't find it right away. Instead, they soon found themselves at the top of Bluff Mountain overlooking a number of rolling hills gradually leading to the peaks of the higher Misty Mountain tops. A thick fog covered the forest floor in the valley, which made it impossible to know what laid beneath the haze.

"These are the great Misty Mountains," Elton realized out loud. "And we are on top of Bluff Mountain."

"Do we have to travel down there and then through all those rolling hills before we reach the summit?" Elaine asked in horror.

"It kinda looks that way. The path only goes in that direction and I'm afraid we're going to have to take the four-wheeler from here and leave the truck."

When they reached the bottom on the other side of Bluff Mountain, they could see what lay ahead. And what they saw made their emotions swell and their heads hurt. Nothing but rough terrain with rocks and rivers and damp canopy covering over head.

They were sitting at the beginning of an empty Unknown Wilderness.

"How could the HeartLand exist here in this place?" Elaine exclaimed in despair.

As the leader, Elton wasn't sure either. But the path continued on, curving away into the dense forest. They decided to continue on their journey moving forward with determination. They rode and they rode over every rock and root, through streams and big puddles. Whenever they got hungry, they'd stop and open the carrier for food. Whenever they got thirsty they'd pull out a drink. Whenever they had to go to the bathroom, they'd hold it hoping just over the next hill there would be a cabin—but that didn't happen—so they had to make do with what they had among the snakes, bears, and other creepy critters. And every time they sang and talked about their Big Dreams of the Inner Longings, they'd just keep on singing and talking.

~

Finally, a lot of time passed. This was not like the fun adventurous times they'd spent before on the four-wheeler. Elton's arms were very tired from holding on to the handlebars, and Elaine's legs were getting chapped. Their faces were wind burned and their bones began to ache. Each day crept into another. They tried to keep each other company but there was no denying the loneliness for family and friends back in Suburb of Soul. And then one day they got hungry along the way when Elaine opened the carrier only to discover... their food was completely gone.

That was the very day when Elton could hardly bear the sad look on his young bride's face. Only, he didn't look at her with the same peaceful compassion he used to... he returned to carrying a heavy burden of despair and resentment, building a wall around his heart. Her dependency on him was taking its toll as he began to regret all the unwanted responsibility.

Out of worry, they called out to Mediator. But they heard nothing. Only the sounds of survival surrounded them as they moved forward.

A day or two later they ran out of drinks from their cooler. They called out to Mediator again ...and again, they heard no reply.

Fortunately, Elton remembered the water purifier he thought to bring even though he didn't think he'd ever need it. They found a trickle of water coming from a rock. At least now they were only starving while the water would keep them alive for a little bit longer. But Elaine knew that if Elton was smart enough to remember the water purifier, as an avid angler, maybe there was some fishing tackle he thought to bring, too.

Sure enough, it wasn't too long before they came across a deep pool beneath a waterfall. While Elton whipped his fly rod through the cool breeze above the serene glassy water, Elaine rejoiced as she noticed some fowl eating some delicious berries in the brush. Rainbow trout stretching from his fingers to his elbow filled the knapsack around his waist. Then Elton, remembering he also brought his twelve-gauge shotgun in case of any trouble, loaded up and began to hunt. He shot one, then two, and the next thing he knew, they had a big meal with fish and fowl roasting over a fire along with baskets full of berries Elaine picked. They ate till they were full.

Still, they hadn't heard from Mediator since they entered the forest.

~

More time passed. The longest lingering minutes of every hour of each day that Elton and Elaine could ever remember passed slowly. Out of desperation, they began to search through every clearing anything that looked like a way out of the forest to the main highway—in spite of the warnings from their good friend, never to do that.

One day, they saw a marker that grabbed their attention with the number 8. It was nailed to a thick and very tall Tulip Poplar tree next to what looked like a shortcut over a ridge. It was Elton's favorite number that represented New Beginnings in the Hebrew language. But to their disappointment, it was only a deer marker leading to a canyon that ended quickly into the thickest brush they'd ever seen.

They even tried traveling at night when the air was cooler. But, in spite of the headlights on the four-wheeler, they kept losing the path.

All the various delays of deep puddles across the path and getting stuck on boulders and fallen trees made them even more determined to get to the big highway. But each and every attempt failed leading to dead end after dead end.

Again and again they'd lose their way and spend all that extra time and energy finding the remnants of the path. They kept crying out to Mediator to show them a better way. But they heard no answers and saw no new signs in sight. Why did they ever abandon their soulish control only to trust their feeble hearts? Why did they allow Mediator to take them out of their comfort zone in the first place, only to come out here and die?

After all the struggle and striving, demanding and bargaining, Elton and Elaine finally came to their wits end. The day came when they finally gave up.

They sat by a big rock and refused to move until Mediator showed them at least a sign or spoke to them about more of the plan.

But Mediator did not reveal His presence in any way shape or form that day. Or the next day. Or the next.

Elton and Elaine had never in all their living days, both in childhood and young adulthood, felt so alone and discouraged and completely without direction. Elaine was beyond frustrated, Elton beyond angry. With protective walls guarding their hearts, they were both bitter and harboring thoughts and feelings that only made them more miserable with each passing moment.

Then a scorching wind out of the east blew through the trees.

~

There was a fire in the forest blowing thick smoke in their eyes, they could hardly breath. Their clothes and hair were full of ash. They found a cave big enough to drive the four-wheeler to safety. Once the harsh winds died down and the threat appeared to blow away, they climbed to a ridge. As far as the eye could see, nothing but a black charred mess of wasteland surrounded them. The path through the forest disappeared completely. No doubt about it in their minds, the entire journey through the forest was a complete waste of time and effort.

Dark black tears streaked down their faces as they held each other in their arms. "You're not to be trusted with our Inner Longings anymore," Elton shouted heavenward. "You're not a bondage breaker, you're a heart breaker. Where's your freedom for freedom sake? It doesn't exist. It's all just a big joke. You promised to be with us wherever we go. You promised to give us our daily bread. Well... you didn't keep your promise! You're not the Provider of blessings or the Giver of gifts we thought you were!"

Elton and Elaine found their way back to the cave and retrieved the four-wheeler and started riding aimlessly across the charred wasteland. Their dream was dead, and now they wanted to die also.

When they came to a flat patch to pitch their tent, they closed their eyes hoping never to wake up again.

That night, they dreamt what seemed like a dreamless sleep for hopeless Seekers and striving Thrivers, without any more Inner Longings of meaning and purpose.

~

Early the next morning, they were both woken by a loud sound of rumblings. Disturbed by the sound, Elaine looked around but nothing was there. Then, after a piece of bark landed in her hair, she looked up and saw something alive in a very tall charred tree. It appeared to be a quiet Commoner perched on a thick branch.

"Who are you?" she asked.

"My name is Joy," the young lady said as she climbed down. "Mediator sent me to help you."

"No way!" shouted Elton. "He had His chance. He abandoned us at the most important time we needed Him. The Dream is gone and I don't want to have anything to do with Inner Longings for my heart ever again."

"Are you sick? Do you have any broken bones? What don't you have that you need?" Joy asked with a quiet voice.

"Well, if it wasn't for me thinking ahead to bring my water purifier, fishing gear, and my shotgun," answered Elton, "we'd surely be dead by now. But we haven't seen streams with fish or fields with fowl for days."

"Ok. And?...," she asked.

"Well, if it weren't for the basket-full of berries I collected, we'd be shriveled up walking skeletons. Oh, wait a minute, we are shriveled up skeletons," Elaine added with sarcasm. "We're about to die of starvation!"

"Hmmm... I see," Joy murmured. "And?..."

"Well," growled Elton, "since you're asking, we're almost out of gas and a little direction would have been nice. We don't know where the heck we are and we don't have a clue as to where we're going now that the path disappeared during the raging fires. Ever since we started out from the washer back at the crossroads, we've run into one obstacle after another without any help. It seems like all we've done is wander around in circles endlessly and completely lost track of time in this wasted Wilderness."

"Oh, I see," Joy said with her head propped on her hand leaning against a tree. "So what's the plan now?"

Furious from the gesture, Elton growled some more, "Just tell us how the heck to get back to the big highway."

"I'm sorry, but I'm not allowed to do that," Joy said. "That, you'll have to do on your own if that's what you choose to do. But I can help you move forward if that is what you still want."

"That figures, Mediator sent us someone who can't compassionately help at our most devastating time of despair," Elaine said with disgust. "You're a Commoner just like us and you can't even find it in you to help out a fellow human being. What good are you, anyway?"

"Considering both your soulish thoughts and emotions, you might be right. That's the choice you have to make. You can either follow your heart or follow your head," Joy humbly acknowledged and made things simple.

Then Joy started walking in a direction Elton thought was absolutely absurd according to his logical thinking and according to Elaine's compass.

~

It wasn't long before Elton started having second thoughts and Elaine changed her mind. Maybe they were wrong for the right reasons for once? Maybe this strange Commoner named Joy wasn't a Commoner at all. Maybe she was a messenger of Mediator actually leading them in the right direction. They shouldn't have been so rude. In fact, something about her confidence and the way she held her Self renewed Elton's hope and Elaine's faith for the first time in a long time.

They both jumped on the four-wheeler and moved forward again, this time to catch up with Joy who disappeared over the hill they would never have chosen.

Once at the top, they were able to scan a new horizon they'd never seen before. The trees below them were green, untouched by the forest fire. Just beyond the valley were another set of hills leading to the peaks of the Misty Mountains.

"Joy!" they both cried out with echoes, but there was no one, not even a faint reply.

"Joy! Joy! Joy!" they shouted over and over. But there was not even a crackling of a twig under foot.

Then Elton had a new idea. He shimmied up one of the tallest charred trees to the very top. He came down quicker than he could think and told Elaine about the new direction they were off to find the path in the forest just ahead by a stream.

Later that same day, while eating fruit from the basket, they talked about how they looked back at their journey through the forest in a whole new light.

"You know?" Elaine spoke up, "I guess I needed to lose a few pounds anyway."

"Yeah, and I needed the exercise because I was getting pretty out of shape back in my comfort zone."

They each belted out a good laugh.

"Joy was right, you know," Elaine added, "we really do have everything we need right now for this very moment. Maybe not for five days from now, but just for right now, today."

"Yeah. And we're back on the path through the forest. I thought we were completely lost until I could actually see through the charred treeeeees...," Elton said with something else in his voice.

"Hey, what are you not telling me?" Elaine suspected.

"Umm... well, I also saw the big highway when I was up in that tree."

How could they have been so blind? Even when the voice of Mediator could not be heard, He had been there all along.

"I knew I could trust you to make the wisest decision, Elton." Elaine said reassuring him of her confidence. "If it was me... I'm pretty sure I would have followed my feelings and entertained all those distracting emotions that want to go back to Suburb of Soul. Thanks."

Unlike other times he'd been impacted on his journey, this was the day when Elton looked at Elaine in a different way. The ice he'd been packing around his heart was finally melting away. He decided he was no longer entitled to think, feel, and act like someone stoic with his emotions. If he was to ever truly love her with unconditional love, it was time to leave his childish, Self-centered ways behind, for good.

One other way they knew Joy was sent from Mediator was when they found, behind a healthy pine tree, three gallons of gasoline, along with a bag of dough, to make biscuits and bread. On the container, she left a note that read:

Elton and Elaine, if you found this gasoline and dough, then you've decided to move forward into the unknown. I hope you never give up on your Big Dream. Just keep on keepin' on until you reach the HeartLand. Until then, may Mediator bless you and keep you safe by His abiding faithfulness to provide and may you always be able to see His provisions even when you can't hear His voice.

— Joy

~

One day, Elton and Elaine met a couple of returning Commoners headed back to Suburb of Soul. They were polite with kind gestures, offering a good word or two of encouragement. But they also told them some very scary stories of things up ahead. Amazingly, they described how they crossed the Unknown Wilderness to the Misty Mountains. Their story was incredible with details giving an account about reaching the Summit, barely making it to a very wide and very deep turbulent river right before the HeartLand. To their dismay, they encountered terrifying creatures so fierce and overwhelming they decided not to stay the course and move forward. They said they felt powerless and helpless, Mediator's voice could no longer be heard or signs seen. But they were happy to be returning to their Perspective Home back in Suburb of Soul.

These returning Commoners in particular sounded very convincing with persuasions of deep convictions. Elton and Elaine immediately recognized their scars as a clear sign of deep wounds inflicted by something they never wanted to come in contact with—even if they do have a gun. Unfortunately, after all they'd been through, apparently these badly wounded Commoners stopped trusting Mediator and lost their Big Dream. And now they were traveling in the opposite direction away from Joy.

The returning Commoners strongly warned them, passionately, what still lay ahead was too hard for any Commoner. But as a consolation, they offered Elton and Elaine another solution that might work. Despite the tempting offer, Elaine looked at Elton and reminded him that they were not the same people... that they had changed. The wilderness had not been a wasteland, but a necessary journey in order for them to overcome their fears in order to strengthen their faith for the Fair Exchange. They were being prepared for what lay ahead, no matter what the cost or how scary the opposition.

"Travel very carefully," Elton and Elaine told the returning Commoners. "There's been a horrible forest fire and the path is impossible to find," they continued to warn them. "As for us, we are going to decline your offer and keep moving forward to the HeartLand no matter the cost."

As Elton and Elaine scurried on their way picking up speed along the path, their hopes from Inner Longings grew stronger than ever. And the more that the heat intensified from the sun overhead, the more Elton and Elaine sang louder their new song and talked the talk of every lesson they'd learned, to remind each other they were going to find the HeartLand and overcome any obstacle, no matter how long it took—as long as they kept in the direction Joy pointed them!

That evening around the campfire, they both solemnly swore to write only the truth from their hearts in their Journey Journals and record all the lessons they had learned. They were seeing things and hearing things through new eyes and new ears that were dull, due to the wall around their hearts. As each layer was peeling away, a renewed faith increased the quality of life in their thoughts, feelings, and actions, especially as their joy increased with favor toward each other and Mediator.

It was that very night when a new revelation came from another dream.

Chapter 7 Journey Journal

This marks the pivotal point for everyone who pursues a conquest of their Inner Longing's Big Dream in the land that the Life Exchanger has *prepared* for all Seekers to travel (Exodus 23:2-33). The backdrop of our story at this point is found in the mountains and valleys of life just beyond our comfort zone. And yet, the reality is we must accept the fact there's also a wilderness we must pass through for good reasons—even though it feels like the worse place on earth we would ever want to be.

But before entering the Forbidden Forest, Elton and Elaine are challenged in their circumstances to look for answers hidden away from the world's philosophies of life. We are told in Scripture (Manual For Life) this is one of the reasons why Mediator spoke in parables. To the average mind, heavenly truths for earthly gain can completely sound mysterious and foreign to the mere mind of man. But these truths *were* meant to be understood, …just not with the soul. They can only be discerned by the human spirit. Not just anyone's spirit, though… only those who have *the* Spirit (Comforter) living within their spirit (1st Corinthians 2)—that is where our new discernment and convictions come from. We are also told that we are not to be caught unaware of the enemy's (Dictator or Rejector) schemes (2nd Corinthians 2:11), who is lurking around seeking those whom he can devour.

Like Elton and Elaine, tried and true, we've been called to follow Mediator to higher ground for wisdom and understanding pertaining to our Big Dreams. Only, this path to higher ground is often difficult terrain found in places we were forbidden to go by our Crazy Makers as well as our enemy—and for good sounding reasons, I might add. Taking a big risk through the Forbidden Forest into unknown territory can sometimes seem very unwise, and even foolish. However, true to human nature needing the Refiner's fire, we must face our wilderness along our journey. In preparation for the Big Dream, the wilderness represents a time for cutting away the old bad habits and worldly conditioning in the flesh.

What do you believe has represented the "wilderness" on your journey so far?

_____

_____

_____

_____

**What do you believe that the word *"prepared"* means in Exodus 23 verse 20, *"and to bring you into the place I have prepared?*

_____

_____

_____

_____

It's certainly our desire to hear the voice of Mediator all the time, right? But there are times when we don't hear His voice at all. It is very important to note that we must look for evidence of His presence and grace, even when we do not hear His voice. Basically, wisdom tells us that if He is in our life at all, then He is in all of our life.

Like the significant provisions for necessities made available to Elton and Elaine even under the most dire conditions (i.e. fishing gear for fish, shotgun for fowl, basket-full of berries, cave for shelter from the fire), what are some of the provisions you know are in your life put there by the Hand of Jehovah Jireh—God your great provider, despite the difficulties you have had to endure?

_____

_____

_____

_____

In Exodus 23 verse 22 we read, *"If you listen carefully to what he (messenger) says and do all that I (the Life Exchanger) say..."* However, did you realize that He sends His messengers (angels) to help his followers on their journey? It is imperative we obey The Life Exchanger and listen to the voice of Mediator— even if the message comes from an unexpected messenger (Joy). There are times we receive direction through angels that come in the form of people. (Hebrews 13:2; 1:14). Even Jesus (Mediator) was ministered to by angels (Matthew 4:10; Mark 1:13)

Can you recall any incidences along your journey where you may have possibly been touched by an angel?

Yes or No If yes, please explain your answer.

_____

_____

_____

_____

There is something we must all be on the look out for when traveling through the forest in the highways and byways of life. Like Elton and Elaine, we run into others like the returning Commoners who apparently chose to end their journey prematurely and go back to their comfort zone in Suburb of Soul. Elton and Elaine actually met others like them earlier in our story while attending Local Gathering.

Who might you think they were and might some of them be on your own personal journey today?

_____

_____

_____

_____

Even though we can relate to the concerns of the returning Commoners in flesh and blood, we are never to listen to "strangers" who try to discourage or even tempt us from moving forward in obedience to the voice of Mediator. As a matter of fact, we are told in 1st John 4 verse 1 that we are to test the spirits around us because there are false prophets among us. What in the world does that look like? In fact, in what way are we supposed to know how to test spirits, let alone discerning the difference between good prophets versus false ones? There is a very clear example in the Old Testament found in the book of 1st Kings chapter 13 verses 11 through 34 illustrating how important it is to stay the course. Listen to the right voice. Do not listen to those who are imposters, who can literally cost you your Big Dream, and even possibly your life.

Interestingly enough, many of us have heard the passage of Scripture in John 10 verse 27, which says, *"My sheep hear My voice, and I know them, and they follow Me."* But back in verses 1 through 5, listen to what Mediator says. *"I tell you the truth, the man who does not enter the sheep pen by the gate, but climbs in by some other way, is a thief and a robber. The man who enters by the gate is the shepherd of his sheep. The watchman opens the gate for him, and the sheep listen to his voice. He calls his own sheep by name and leads them out. When he has brought out all his own, he goes on ahead of them, and his sheep follow him because they know his voice. But they will never follow a stranger; in fact, they will run away from him because they do not recognize a stranger's voice."*

Notice three very important issues facing the sheep (followers): 1) There are bad shepherds who try to enter the fold through other means, climbing over the hedge of protection; 2) there is a gate where there is a gatekeeper; and 3) the good shepherd's sheep will never follow a stranger's voice, but will in fact, run away because they do not recognize their voice.

Can you relate to this warning in your current situation?   Yes or No
If yes, please describe it:

_____

_____

_____

_____

Chapter 8

The Language of The Innermost Being

———⟨⟩———

That night, while Elton was sleeping, he dreamed about a majestic being standing near his bed from a balcony wearing a beautiful flowing royal gown blowing in the wind.

"Well done, Elton." the voice said. "I have heard you speak the language of your heart to mine. Welcome to the sanctuary of Innermost Being where the abundance of your Inner Longings are full of Peace and Joy and will keep you safely balanced for the rest of your life. You have spoken to me in the Language of the heart few ever speak. Like most Commoners, you used to only express your thoughts and emotions from your soul to express meaning and purpose with other Commoners, especially in your covenant with Elaine."

"Is it wrong for Elaine and I to relate with our thoughts and emotions in our souls?" Elton asked the One.

"No, not at all." the One said. "What is wrong, and what is to your dismay, is when you rely only on your thoughts and emotions to dictate your choices. That is why you struggle having Thankfulness toward Elaine. The Manual For Life has warned you not to live the way of the flesh."

"So what are we supposed to do with our thoughts and emotions if they cause us to make such bad fleshly decisions?"

"Thoughts and feelings have never caused anyone to make bad fleshly decisions. The bad decisions begin with *disbelief*, which leads to *disobedience*. As you have heard it said many times before, it is not about *doing*, it is about *being*!"

"So is it wrong to try to do the right thing with our thoughts and emotions?" Elton was perplexed. "Just when I think I get it, I really get more confused about this *be* to *do* thing."

"Elton," the One spoke with a direct tone, "recall the many lessons you have learned on your journey. Isn't there one lesson above all the rest? What is indicative of your new *Identity* abounding in your heart is to govern your mind and your body so that Self won't continue to be defined by the performance-based system—or control your behavior by the flesh. Once again, you are no longer to live a soulish life in the flesh, but a new life in the Spirit."

"So, why am I continuing to make big mistakes, especially with Elaine?" Elton asked with a defeated yet defensive tone in his voice.

"As you recall," the One answered, "you cared for your Self more than others by trying to manipulate, meeting your needs your way. At first, you pursued Elaine Selfishly. That is what all Self-seeking Commoners do. You couldn't help but have unrealistic expectations, thus, she was only going to let you down. Unfortunately, you took her shortcomings personally as if it was a reflection on your own Self. However, since you've left Suburb of Soul, I've watched you grow from the inside-out as a Seeker and Thriver, willing to be Self-sacrificing through unconditional love. Now, from deep beneath your soul, your heart has learned to deny indulging your Flesh. With great pleasure to my heart, you have humbled yourself and have been willing to sacrifice so much. Great is your reward to become a Connector if you stay the course. My desire is to share my glory with you and Elaine in a covenant of love through the Fair Exchange. I have something very special for both of you just up ahead. Keep the faith, stay on the path, and know that I am with you, always."

~

When Elton awoke, he was laying beside a bubbling brook stretched out on a flat rock. How he got there, or what persuaded him, he didn't have a clue. All he knew was an intuitive sense coming from inside—so mysterious but delightfully inviting. His Inner Longings were once again permeating every fiber of his being.

And then, he felt a touch. Elaine was sitting beside him gently stroking his right arm.

Still half asleep, he wondered if what was happening at the moment was simply a silly fantasy, or was he visited by Mediator again in a dream. Nevertheless, he relished the moment with Elaine and the strong thoughts and feelings he knew were perfectly pure because they were now speaking to each other with the language of the heart. But still, he couldn't help but wonder if Mediator was *really* pleased with him and if He found favor with Him. And, he even wondered, no matter how many miles of wilderness behind them, would this deeper heart connection of communication really last between he and Elaine despite all their differences?

~

The morning sun grew brighter through the trees, and they decided it was time to get on their way again. This time the path followed beside a stream for miles as if something seemed to be drawing them upward. If it was anything like his dream, it felt like another invitation.

Before long, enormous-sized boulders towered up from the floor of the forest where they had fallen from the cliffs above. Weaving in and out of them, Elton and Elaine felt like birds flying on their four-wheeler through a rock forest. The moment quieted their spirits and captured the essence of their meaning and purpose. Words only spoken from a language within the Innermost Being comforted their hearts.

Then the path began to ascend higher and higher far above the stream below, until suddenly they entered a level clearing overcome by the brightness of the sun.

The language of their hearts told them this was a very special place and they were in the presence of the Life Exchanger.

"Follow the path a little farther," they heard His voice clearly ringing in their heart.

Their eyes beheld a scene their lips could not express. Like a tropical paradise nestled in the mountains, there was a waterfall cascading into a deep blue pool where the mist climbed high into the sky covering the peaks with rainbow colors.

"Come, my good and faithful servants, and taste the water," the voice spoke again. "Do not be afraid, for I am with you. Take a dip and refresh your weary bodies in the coolness of the water,"

Elton and Elaine held each other's hand and slipped into the most spectacular Eden-like garden they could have ever imagined. They dove and they swam, they floated and they splashed, frolicking like they had all the time in the world. Nowhere else to be. No one else to be with. Just the five of them, Elaine, Elton, Mediator, Life Exchanger, and Comforter; unlocking the spiritual chambers of the Innermost Being of their hearts, freeing them from the bondage of flesh.

Time passed even though the concept of time and space eluded these Seekers. They were being transformed by the renewing of their minds as they were finally coming into the fullness of their Identity in Mediator. Their personalities became vivacious as their temperaments were released with new freedom of expression. Gifts, talents, and abilities became alive with creativity more than they could have ever grasped all their potential before. Their Inner Longings knowingly experienced the essence of their meaning and purpose with visions, aspirations, and enthusiastic ambitions!

After their swim and frolicking ended near the waters edge, both Elaine and Elton realized that this clean washing from all the soot and ash on the path through the forest was well overdue. No one could make the journey without a good washing from the past. But this wasn't just a mere bathing for their bodies. This was a cleansing through and through, their whole spirit, soul, and body—especially the soul from all the Self-flesh crud.

~

They decided, with the Life Exchanger's permission, to stay and relax for a few more days. His favor had never felt so real and wonderful along with a peace that surpassed all understanding, guarding their hearts and minds. There was a language of love and grace tying a noose around their spirits with renewed hope. They were ultimately released from all the old performance-based acceptance, connected to the faulty system of man-made rules and regulations.

After dinner one evening, in the stillness of a quiet moment, they heard His voice say, "Elaine, come into the light."

At that very moment is when Elaine stood and walked toward a mid-size tree with beautiful fruit hanging from the branches. The light from the tree not only shown all around, but radiated through her soul. Elaine didn't realize it, but Elton noticed from behind her the light shining through her, he was drawn like a moth to a flame.

Trembling inside, they each looked at their Self and could see something had changed. They were different creatures inside with new natures, reshaped by a new understanding. There was wisdom that wasn't there before. They felt safe for the very first time, uninhibited and unafraid to be transparent. However, there were also things revealed by the light that were not attractive about Self in the souls of both of them. Things that were down right embarrassing they did not want each other to see. But neither one acted startled, or laughed, or turned their eyes away from the other. No more fear, shame, guilt, or pain that normally led to rejection. They only had a healthy sense of love, trust, respect, acceptance, and hearts wide open for the *Fair Exchange.*

The light exposed all the Self-Centeredness and Self-Condemnation of the sin-scarred soulish life. There were all the things they had said and done out of: Selfishness, Self-Justifying, Self-Introspection, Self-Serving, Self-Pity, Self-Pride, Self-Determination, Self-assuredness, Self-Confidence, Self-Consciousness, Self-Satisfaction, Self-Deception, Self-Denial, Self-Indulgent, Self-Gratifying, Self-Righteous, Self-Motivated, Self-Sufficient, Self-Taught and Self-Made people. Self, Self, Self, Self... it was all they could take. Absolutely disgusting with a stench neither could bear.

And yet, instead of these things having anymore power to create more darkness, the Life Exchanger revealed them in the light of His Son in order to purge them out and render the deeds of the *flesh* dead—washing them clean of the unseen filth from Self's illusion of control.

With tears coming down their faces from all the overwhelming thoughts and feelings, Elton said, "I am wretched and unworthy, I am sincerely sorry for being a sinner. Please, by your grace, have mercy, take away this filth from within me, do not leave me empty and void, exchange it with only the goodness of You that I may not perish from your presence!"

Elaine, just as repentant of those same sentiments, added, "And I too am ugly and impure. I am truly sorry for being a sinner. I give it all to you. Please, by your grace, I want to be exchanged for life. Cleanse my whole being in the pure waters of the pool so you can look upon me with favor and delight, pleasing in your sight by the light of your life and glory!"

The Life Exchanger had already supernaturally done just that at the moment of their salvation. But this was about sanctification. Though they never presumed it, He exchanged the righteousness of Mediator for their old nature, already. While they were still yet sinful Commoners on earth, He gave His abundance of new life. And yet, the new nature was not about Self at all, it was centered in His Holy Identity full of tender mercies showcasing the glory of His peaceful presence.

Elton and Elaine had become the righteousness of Mediator by his divine providence. Their heavenly bridegroom spoke these encouraging words to His covenant bride, "According to my gospel of grace, I've forgiven you as far as the East is from the West, and as deep as the deepest sea! From now on, know that you are the salt and light of the earth with a strength nothing can overshadow or thwart my will. You are the apple of my eye. I want you to know that I am pleased with you, your debt has been paid in full. I am pleased that you have received by faith what I have done for you. You are completely pardoned and have overcome the things of this world. Through my gift, you are made complete and can do all the things I command you by the power I have vested in you. You are no longer *wretched* or *impure*. Rather, by the cleansing of your Innermost Being, you have been made righteous and free, through and through, your whole spirit, soul, and body. Remember from this day forward, I have heard your repentant hearts. Out of my very own personal workmanship, I have sculpted a good work in you, and you are no longer of the old in Adam. You have a new nature. You are Victorious! Super-conquerors! Ready for the mission I have set before you. But it is not some-thing you are to ever accomplish on your own... I must live *through* you. I stand at the door and knock. Hear my voice and never build a wall of protection. I will walk with you, talk with you, laugh and dine with you. You will know my voice, and follow me. I will never abandon you or disown you because you are a part of me—for I cannot disown myself. You are to partake of my divine nature. I will be with you always. And yet, one thing I ask of you again... even though there are many difficulties to come, do not build a wall around your heart for any reason at all. Only guard your heart with the armor of my protection."

~

The next day the Life Exchanger called to them again, "Come closer to me by my Spirit and through the wisdom found in the Manual For Life so I can validate your true value and worth along with your meaning and purpose. You now have eyes to see and ears to hear what has been made complete by me in my Son, the Tree of Life. Eat. Drink. Have all the abundance of Life I am offering you, by Grace! Never depart, and always drink from the well with rivers of living water, which is Comforter."

This went on and on for a few more days until Elaine and Elton were washed pure, through and through—white like snow. The cleaner they got, the more their Innermost Being became connected with their Inner Longings.

One more time the Life Exchanger called them to Himself at another place. This time to a high Tower of Power at the top of the majestic Misty Mountains.

~

Elton and Elaine gathered all their stuff and headed up to the summit of the mountain. The further they went, the more they felt one with each other and Mediator. They could hardly wait to find out what the Life Exchanger had in store for them at the Tower of Power.

Before long, they made it to the summit. Without needing to be told, Elton and Elaine began to climb the stairs up and up until they were standing on the Platform of Surrender, high above the treetops. Gazing out at the absolutely breathtaking vista, the glorious sight was more than they could fathom with their minds or behold with their emotions.

"Just as I promised, the HeartLand is here for you just as it has been for millenniums before you," the Life Exchanger said.

"I can see it! We made it!" Elaine shouted with sheer joy. "The HeartLand for our Big Dream is right over there."

"Take note, you will never be ambitious for what you don't value," His powerful voice continued, "ambition begins when you perceive the value of your Inner Longings true meaning and purpose and express it with the spiritual language of your heart. Up until your journey, you mistakenly loved the glory that comes from man in the performance-based system more than the freedom given by me for freedom sake. Your search for man's approval is over. Now your ambition for real meaning and purpose can begin." Then after a pause, "Elton and Elaine...," said the Life Exchanger.

"Yes," they said in unison.

"Give me your Inner Longings."

"What do you mean?" Elton asked. "I received them in return from the great exchange. They are the grace-gifts of my Inner Longings you gave to me, right? I mean, they are mine now."

"Yes, and now I am asking you to give them back to me."

~

Elton paced back and forth around the perimeter of the Platform of Surrender while Elaine just sat in the middle. Neither could understand this new demand of the Life Exchanger after all that had happened. Why would He want to take back their Inner Longings? How were they to express the language of their hearts without them? Did they *do* something wrong? This didn't make sense. It didn't feel right. How were they to go on and complete the journey of their Big Dream without the inner source of their driving force, they wondered. Especially now, when they had come so far to reach the summit.

Then Elaine had a feeling. Maybe she could still bargain. "Do we really have to give our Inner Longings back, or is this just a test?"

"No," the Life Exchanger replied, "you do not *have* to give them back. Some, like the couple you met returning to Suburb of Soul, chose not to."

"So we have a choice," Elton proclaimed. "We can keep our Inner Longings if we want to?" But instead of enjoying the idea, he felt sad and confused as if he was disobeying the One. What were they going to do?

He sat down in the middle of the platform next to Elaine. "Remember what that couple said? They encountered terrible creatures so fierce and overwhelming that they felt powerless and helpless. And Mediator's voice could not be heard or any signs seen."

"Yeah," Elaine replied, "and maybe the reason why they felt powerless and helpless is because they did not give their Inner Longings back to the Life Exchanger? There was something about them I didn't trust from the moment we met them."

"Very Good!" the Life Exchanger validated Elaine. "They tried to get you to do it on your own a different way. Unfortunately, they held on to what I had given them... as their own. As false Thrivers, they lost the vision, and the fierceness of the terrible creatures turned their anger on me by trying to deceive you."

But there was still a choice.

Time passed. They thought and thought some more pondering all the possibilities. The choice was breaking free their heart in a new and different way as they felt the need to make a decision without answers. The sun set and rose again. But this time they remembered the poem from their original dream: *A shroud of clouds hide dusk's beauty, while hope slips quietly into the night. But rising from dawn's visual feast, a promise comes with new light. You already know what you want to do, but you don't know how to do what you know. Soon you'll leave the comfort of your home, when the time comes, you must go. Your answer lies beyond the hills, in a land you cannot see. Find the friend you already know, a new Connector he will be.*

"That's it!" Elton exclaimed in excitement. "Don't you see, Elaine, we have to let go and stop clinging to our Inner Longings the way we desired approval in the performance-based system. No longer Seeking for meaning and purpose in and of our Self?"

"Umm... sorry, but that's not a news flash. My dilemma is still, why?"

"Don't you see? They were never ours in the first place," Elton continued, "they've always been the Life Exchanger's. It's not up to us to *do* anything with them. We are meant to give back to Him any right or entitlement we thought we had to hold on to them for our Self. If we give them back, He will complete the mission He set before us... in and through us!"

"Yeaaaah... it's becoming clearer to me now!" Elaine exclaimed. "He had to change something *in* us so He could do something *with* us. In fact, He had to do all these things *to* us in order to do something *through* us, no matter how long it took or what havocs it might bring."

"Fantastic!" the voice of the Life Exchanger rang out. "As it is written in the Manual For Life, apart from Mediator, you can do nothing of any eternal worth and value. He must be the one to complete the good work I began in you. All I need from you is a teachable and approachable heart, clinging to me for all you are worth. Like every good follower, when you are teachable, you are reachable. When you are approachable, you are coachable. Now, you must go the rest of your journey with the Connector I have provided for you in the HeartLand."

"Hey, I bet it's your dear old friend Kindred-Spirit, he's the new Connector," Elaine said.

"I bet you're right," said Elton.

~

In the morning, they climbed down the Platform of Surrender from the top of Tower of Power. When they reached the bottom, there was a very unique perfectly round stone just randomly lying on the ground. Elton picked it up. "Wow, this stone is so smooth, almost like the perfect skipping stone. I used to love skipping stones with my dad."

It felt really good fitting perfectly in the palm of his hand. He turned it over and they both noticed at the same time it had the word etched on the other side: BELIEVE.

"Who was it for?" they wondered and pondered. "What did it mean? Was it for them from the Life Exchanger or put there by another Seeker? What were they to believe?" they both thought the same thoughts.

Placing the stone in Elaine's right hand, Elton asked her to hold it. Elaine tried to remember back. Maybe it was from Joy. What would she say to them now? Or maybe the returning Commoner's, the couple with such deep despair and false hope in their eyes. "There's no way they could have surrendered their Inner Longings—they displayed no more trust in Mediator," Elaine thought to herself. She placed the stone back in Elton's hands.

Finally, his thoughts turned back toward the Life Exchanger. Despite the anguish of learning hard lessons, The Life Exchanger's Son, Mediator, never let them down. He had always kept His promises. He had always been good to Elton, in spite of his unhealthy perception.

Then, with their hearts connected, they both knew what they had to do—no, what they had to *be*, in order to *do*.

They made their way back to the four-wheeler and pulled out the Manual For Life along with their Journey Journals. With their Swiss Army knife-pens, they began to write down all the wisdom of truth their eyes could now see in total agreement with what the Life Exchanger had told them. Amazingly, they observed so much more about the spiritual nature of the language of the heart from the Manual For Life. The memory of their minds now had been renewed according to their new perspective. Words and phrases, jumping off the pages, had new meaning they'd never embraced before. With no more performance treadmills, the Manual For Life was no longer the letter of the law, it was actually living and alive by the Spirit of the law—dividing between soul and spirit, examining the thoughts and attitudes of their hearts.

~

Later that day, they reached another very wide and deep flowing river. This river had no bridge. There was no tunnel or way around. And... there were no turbulent waters they'd been warned about. They had no plan or strategy as to how they'd cross it, but that didn't matter, they had each other, and were determined to be obedient. Whatever they would face from here on out, they knew the importance of clinging to the Life Exchanger together by faith. Even when they couldn't hear Mediator's voice, they continued to abide in the truth of the Manual For Life by Comforter.

Then, someone near the waters edge approached them.

"Hello," Elton said. "Who are you?"

"My name is Peace, and The Life Exchanger sent me to help you cross the river to the other side."

"Thank you, for sure," Elaine expressed her gratitude. "We were just trying to figure that out. So, is there a bridge not far from here?"

"No. There's no bridge. Funny, it's always interesting meeting Seekers after they've been to the Tower of Power. You see, this is the place where everyone must apply faith with courage according to what you've already learned. Follow me and I will show you the way. Oh, and by the way, you will need your BELIEVE stone."

Miraculously, Peace skipped her own stone across the river, and then walked on the water all the way to the other side. "Now, skip your stone on the water before you attempt to cross." She shouted before entering the Forest through the path.

Were they supposed to leave their four-wheeler and walk the rest of the way like Peace did? They never walked on water before. Maybe they would have to swim.

Then, Elton noticed a mound of stones piled next to the path on the other side where Peace disappeared.

A little to Elaine's surprise, Elton took from his pocket the Stone, skipped it across the river, and after it reached the other side, he then began slowly driving the four-wheeler into the water, following it's path. Even though a four wheeler's larger balloon tires can normally sustain its own weight for floating, the combined wait of Elton and Elaine would surely make it sink. Nevertheless, Elton boldly followed the ripples made by the stone. They never sank. They didn't even get stuck.

"Hey Elton, the stone seemed to pick exactly the right spot where the river was smooth and shallow enough to cross," Elaine gleamed.

But, when they crawled along more than fifteen feet from the shore where they began, it became more than obvious a miraculous experience was taking place, to say the least. They could see how deep and wide the river really was once they drove over the middle. There were yard-long fish swimming deep beneath them and big rocks way down below. By faith they trusted this incredible experience, which they could not fathom with their mere mind.

But something else happened inside both of their hearts. Their eyes saw new colors and their ears heard new sounds.

When they reached the other side, they found another note placed on the pile of stones. This time, it was from their new friend Peace.

Elton and Elaine, the Life Exchanger is giving you back your Inner Longings. He now knows He can trust you not

to ever cling to them or use them apart from Him, ever again. Now you will achieve great things together by the Fair Exchange as you keep one another Accountable. Remember, He is with you always!

   Peace

The Life Exchanger's favor toward them was more gracious, more wonderful, more trustworthy than they could ever comprehend or express. They wept together with tears of joy as they held each other by the bank of the river.

Something was very different as they received back their Inner Longing's, speaking the spiritual language of their hearts. The urgings grew bigger than ever before. It wasn't about their Self, though, it was about the world around them and the eternal significance of their existence for Mediators glory. They wanted to shout from the top of the world!

Just as Common Sense had told Elton a long time ago, the path through the Forest was just a stone's throw away. Now he understood exactly what he meant. In front of the path entering the Forest, there was a sign that read:

YOU ARE NOW ENTERING THE HEARTLAND
TEACH YOUR CHILDREN WHAT TOOK PLACE HERE

At the entrance, they observed the mound of round flat stones piled high nice and neat, each stone from others who made it to this point and beyond. Every one of them had the word BELIEVE etched on them. Elton took their stone and placed it on the pile. While standing at the threshold of the path, an awesome reverence toward the Life Exchanger flooded Elaine with a peace, accompanied by feelings of safety and security. All of her needs were provided for. She was now challenged by faith in what was to come.

Strangely, they both sensed deep in their Innermost Being a presence of many other witnesses, as they were now part of the Remnant who overcame the temptation to keep their Inner Longings for their Self.

The path to the HeartLand was more narrow than it had ever been before. In spectacular fashion, the trees were greener and many of them had an abundance of fruit. Through the laughing ripples clapping against rocks, there was a stream parallel with the path from here forward. Plenty of fish to eat. An endless supply of water to drink. There were meadows with cabins already built, furnished so they could sleep under warm, dry shelter at night.

All was well as they anticipated a union of fellowship with their Connector, soon.

Chapter 8 Journey Journal

Unfortunately, most believers, according to a poor Identity in Mediator, have not been baptized in the cleansing waters from all the soulish Self-flesh crud, and stood by the Tree of Life where the light exposes everything. Too often we depend on all our scheduled meetings with rituals and customs from professional ministers to validate and affirm us. But all followers of the faith in truth and love (according to the Manual For Life) have direct access to the Life Exchanger through Mediator, who is the propitiation for our sins, not the baptism bath tubs or confessional booths.

We all must hear the voice of the One who holds the power and authority to declare each follower righteous and holy. There are so many who quote a phrase from the Bible that is not in the Bible anywhere: "We're sinners saved by grace." That is a false statement. In fact, the truth is that believers *were* sinners who have been saved by grace and are now saints. But we still have flesh and the choice to give into sin's temptations. That's why we are more accurate to say: we are saints that sin.

What is your personal belief according to the Bible (Manual For Life) regarding your status with God (the Life Exchanger)?

_____

_____

_____

_____

According to Ephesians chapter three, the Holy Spirit lives in our Innermost Being and Jesus lives in our heart. We also learn from the Manual For Life that the Life Exchanger cleanses us (children of light) from all sin by the blood of Mediator, His son (1st John 1:7); we not only become the righteousness of the

Life Exchanger (2nd Corinthians 5:21), we are the functioning Temple of the Holy spirit (1st Corinthians 6:19).

Like Elton and Elaine, have you experienced hearing the voice of the Life Exchanger affirm and validate your new Identity? Yes or No Please explain your answer.

_____

_____

_____

_____

The Spirit begins from within our hearts and permeates every fiber of our being, right? *"He who believes in Me, as the <u>Scripture</u> said, From his <u>inner-most</u> being will flow rivers of living water. By this He meant the Spirit" John 7:38-39a;* The Holy Spirit convicts (John 16:8), regenerates (Titus 3:5), baptizes (Eph. 4:4-5), indwells (1st Cor. 3:16), and fills up (Eph. 5:18), guaranteeing redemption (Eph. 1: 13-14). He comforts by God's Word. (John 14:26; 16:13).

Every Seeker and Thriver has been given gifts, talents, and abilities expressed through love not natural to this world. And because the supernatural presence of Mediator and Comforter live in the new heart of every believer, this spiritual language spoken of in the Manual For Life must be used to communicate our heart. In fact, we are empowered supernaturally in a dimension that is spiritual by nature. Unfortunately, many either completely miss this out of ignorance or simply refuse to be yielded due to fear.

I believe most is out of fear. Here's why.

The #1 manifestation of the Comforter above all else is perfect love. Thankfully, according to 2nd Corinthians 5:14, all believers, having died to the old Adam when we died with Mediator, are no longer to live for themselves. Rather, we are to be totally compelled by the perfect love now in our heart. As a matter of fact, because the Life Exchanger has bestowed this perfect love in us, in 1st John

178

chapter 4 we learn that greater is He (Mediator) who lives in us, than he (Rejector) who lives in the world. Those who are from the world only speak the language of the world, and only listen to each other—not us. Because they don't listen to us, they are not of the Life Exchanger.

Ok, to answer the last line of questioning in the previous chapter, this is exactly how we discern between the spirit of truth from the spirit of error in others.

Let's get real, the Life Exchanger is love. It is by perfect love that we know Him and are now made complete in Him. Therefore, we are now to speak the language of the heart by the way we love Him and one another. This is how we are newly equipped with supernatural grace-gifts and perfected by Him through the way we love one another. By this we have confidence that perfect love casts our fear. Any one who is afraid of punishment and pain is not made complete in perfect love. It's as simple as that.

So, if you claim to have been made complete in perfect love, are the spiritual grace-gifts being manifest in and through you? Yes or No Please explain your answer specifically in the evidence of the manifestations.

_____

_____

_____

_____

At the Tower of Power on the Platform of Surrender where Elton and Elaine were to give back their Inner Longings to The Life Exchanger, why do you believe it is so hard for all of us to process that part of the exchange?

_____

_____

_____

_____

What is it that you are still holding on to as if it is yours to keep and yours to do with what you want?

_____

_____

_____

_____

Like the Israelites who crossed the Red Sea to travel through the wilderness in order to cross the Jordan River by faith into the Promised Land, Elton and Elaine found their journey at the waters edge needing directions for the HeartLand. The most important aspect of this historical account is to notice how accurately human nature is captured at each stage. At this stage of our journey, we are challenged to be honest about our own willingness to walk by faith when entering the Heartland, especially knowing that there are terrible creatures we have to face.

What are your greatest hesitancies for skipping the stone across the river in order to enter the narrower path?

_____

_____

_____

_____

Chapter 9

The Terrifying Creatures

The next morning, as the air glittered from a foggy mist melting in the morning sun, Elton and Elaine entered a wide grassy meadow sprinkled with dew, leaving a remnant of footprints leading to a gate. Soon, followed by a pattern of tire tracks, they came upon a sign that read:

SEEKERS
BEWARE OF THE
TERRIFYING CREATURES

They stared at the sign in a bit of a quandary and horror, wondering if they may have missed a turn behind them. But they realized in this moment of reality, the returning Commoners were right about one thing, the terrifying creatures were very real.

They felt a *little* safe with Elton's shotgun riding in the carrier in case of danger. Other than that, they had no weapons to match the size of terrifying creatures according to the reports from others. From their vantage point, they had no plans for taking on terrifying creatures without the help of Mediator. Plus, their

Big Dream for Inner Longings was bigger than ever. They trusted Mediator to keep His promise and show them the way to the HeartLand.

So they pressed on.

~

Elton and Elaine hadn't gone far when they heard a very strange sound. Elton grabbed his gun while they scurried to find a place to hide. They in no way were ready to face terrifying creatures... yet!

But when Elton and Elaine peered from behind a boulder, they didn't see big hairy grizzly bears or ghoulish werewolves, but a mighty warrior that looked like a glowing angelic being inside a suit of armor with big bulging muscles and a deep booming voice.

"Come out where I can see you, Combat Soldier!" the mighty warrior stood his ground.

Elton had only moments to think, though he never suspected what was to come next. "You talking to me?" He finally asked in a meager squeaky voice.

"Of course you, and the other one too who's hiding behind that boulder with you."

"I'm no Combat Soldier. Certainly no match for a terrifying creature like you," Elton said trembling in great terror, as he and Elaine crawled out from behind the boulder. He'd never felt so weak and fearful. "I'm just a surviving Commoner from Suburb of Soul, and this is my partner, Elaine" he said.

"Nonsense!" as the earth shook from his enormous boot hammering the ground. "Every Seeker from Suburb of Soul who dares come this far is no longer a surviving Commoner, but a Combat Soldier," the warrior said. "As for me? I'm the Gatekeeper of the HeartLand. No one passes through or around the gate without my permission. It is Mediator's request that I assist Combat Soldiers, not Commoners. Why would you be so terrified of these measly terrifying creatures?"

"Because they are much bigger than us with more dangerous weapons than we can afford," Elaine squeamishly answered.

"With a defeatist attitude like that, surely you are defeated already. Why come and do battle if you believe you and your weapons are so small?"

Neither Elton nor Elaine had a good answer to that response. In avoidance, Elton asked, "So you are not one of the terrible creatures?"

"Of course not," the booming voice sent chills down their spine. "I am here to show Combat Soldiers like you the way to the community of others who are your strength in numbers. However, you must be courageous and fear not so you can defeat the terrifying creatures that want to stand in your way."

"He did? Mediator sent you to help fight the terrifying creatures?" Elaine asked with her thoughts focused on one thing, then turning toward Elton. "You *do* need some help, Elton," she said to her partner.

"What do you mean *I* need some help? I thought we were in this together? You know… we, us, our, together? What happened to the Fair Exchange?" Elton barked back at her. Then he said to the Gatekeeper, "Compared to these terrifying creatures, I'm just a meager engineer with degrees …and not very impressively good at that. I've never been trained for combat in the armed forces to fight battles against huge enemies. I am the least of my family, who is of the least of our community, located in the least part of our town among the fortunes of few."

"You're perfect for the job! But you underestimate your strength and training, Combat Warrior," the Gatekeeper said. "Size does not matter in the battles you will face against these terrifying creatures. All your degrees do not matter, either. You must rely on Mediator's provisions and the lessons you have learned on your journey, together. You and your partner are to be one. As you have read in the Manual For Life, how can two walk on the same path if they are not in agreement? …Two are stronger than one against their opposition, they are to have a

Fair Exchange with hearts wide open in a community of Seekers." He paused for a moment. "But don't get me wrong, the terrifying creatures are very real, and very terrifying. They're intimidatingly enormous even for me… if I was to face them in my own strength! They will try to stand in the way of your Inner Longings. But if you believe in Mediator and willing to continue to take a big risk… you *will* stand your ground and defeat them."

"But we have no skills or abilities acquired for this kind of battle," Elaine cried out. "We have no big weapons or thick armor to protect our Selves."

In a gentler tone from the towering giant, "You do not need to protect your *Self*, pretty one. Only Guard your heart with the armor of Mediator." Then the Gatekeeper sat on a boulder continuing to explain about all the recent steps and stages of their journey where Mediator had been preparing their hearts—*not* Self—and equipping them for what's ahead. "Only abide in the Truth you've learned on your journey," he said, "It is the Truth that makes you free and keeps you free for freedom sake."

"But how will we know what to do?" Elton asked. "We have learned lessons but we don't have the practical wisdom to apply them, yet."

"Apparently your flesh is stronger than I thought. Have you not learned, yet?" The patience of the Gatekeeper was growing thin. "It is not about what your flesh continues to want to *do*, it's about who your heart is meant to *be*! Mediator has already given you exactly what you need in order for Him to do His work *through* you—spirit, soul, and body. You simply are to yield your True Identity to Him and rely upon His faithfulness to finish what He began in you."

Elton and Elaine looked at each other with a sense of reassurance. But neither one were convinced they were Combat Soldiers.

"Beware! Do not justify disobedience, Elton and Elaine," the Gatekeeper said matter-of-factly. "Disobedience is due to Unbelief. Unbelief is far more dangerous than any of the terrifying creatures, which leads to the temptation to rebuild a wall of protection around your heart, resorting back to the performance-based system for approval. Like before, if you allow the Wall Builders a foothold, they will take full advantage and create strongholds. If that happens, you will not be able to hear the voice of Mediator when it comes time to following His lead in fighting the terrifying creatures!"

"Oh, so that's what happened in the past?..." Elaine asked with a smirky statement. Then, with a smug look on her face, "Think pretty girls with flattering tongues or successful men with big bank accounts could have anything to do with it?"

"Oh, like you're any different from me?" Elton barked back. "And I thought we shared that stuff in complete confidence? I trusted you, and now you use it against me at your convenience. Manipulator! How could you do that Elaine? That hurts real deep," Elton rebuttaled like a schoolboy.

The Gatekeeper just shook his head, then pointed the way they were to go and did not move from his seat. "Just keep on the path on the other side of the meadow where you will be greeted by a friend. I will remain here to protect you from the wolves-in-sheep's-clothing who try to sneak their way around the gate, those thieves and robbers are not far behind you now.

~

They hadn't gone far past the gate into the forest when they met their first terrifying creature. It was gigantic, all right! Overshadowing the path, it completely blocked them from moving forward with their Inner Longings.

Barely glancing in their direction, the creature took a deep sigh, asking, "And what were you thinking you were going to do, small Commoners?"

Elton looked at Elaine sarcastically, "This certainly is not a friend." Then glancing back at the hideous enemy named Loneliness.

185

"You're exactly right, Elton. But you're not alone." A voice came from behind them. Both Elton and Elaine turned to look. It was their Connector, Kindred-Spirit.

"Oh Kindred-Spirit, are we ever glad to see you," Elaine said.

They exchanged hugs and endearing smiles of pleasure. "You both look fantastic for having come this far." Kindred-Spirit complemented. "I am so proud of you both for sticking together this long. It is hard enough for just one Seeker to make it this far... but partners?... let me tell ya, that is a feat within itself. So what do you think and how do you feel about what you're going to do with this terrifying creature, Loneliness?"

Elaine grinned, "No, you're not going to trick us with that one. If there's one thing I've learned from our journey away from Suburb of Soul, we should not be manipulated by thoughts and feelings for *doing* ever again."

"Very good. I'm impressed," the wise Connector said. "I'm surprised you were able to catch that so quickly," he said congratulating Elaine. "Ok. Now that you are advanced in wisdom and understanding, the practical applications require learning *Exchanged For Life discipleship*. That's what I'm here for. As your Heart Connector, I will be mentoring you along the way according to the Manual For Life. Your part? You will conquer each and every terrifying creature, together."

"But Kindred-Spirit," Elton interrupted. "I'm confused about there being terrifying creatures here. I thought Mediator already cleaned out the bad from HeartLand and now you were to help us replace it with good?"

"Yes, that is partially true," Kindred Spirit hesitated to give the complete answer.

"But this is the HeartLand, the safest place on earth? There shouldn't be any terrifying creatures, right?" Elton suggested with assumption.

"That's a common misconception from false impressions, which lead to unrealistic expectations," Kindred-Spirit said setting the record straight. "Try to understand, those are common mistakes most Seekers make with preconceived notions taught from unhealthy interpretations of the Manual For Life," Kindred-Spirit continued speaking while sitting down. "I can appreciate your optimism with hopeful anticipation about the HeartLand, but be careful not to read too much into Mediator's promise that comes with True Identity. Finding your new identity was almost like becoming a believer all over again, wasn't it? Once you became a Seeker and Thriver, your mind in your soul has needed a continuous renewing to break the old patterns conformed by Suburb of Soul's conditioning. Unfortunately, the soul is where so many become disillusioned by unrealistic expectations. Remember, you were taught unhealthy values and beliefs back at your Local Gathering. You must unlearn the old stinkin' thinkin' in order to relearn right believing."

"So the HeartLand is *not* a safe place?" Elaine questioned with despair in her voice.

"Oh no, my dear child. On the contrary. The HeartLand *is* the safest place on earth! But it is not the heavenly paradise above. It is the Kingdom of God and His righteousness in your heart here on earth—the Kingdom of Heaven within." Connector constantly spoke in words reflecting the Manual For Life. "If you're looking for the perfect paradise, you'll have to keep waiting till you ascend into the next dimension of eternity."

"Wow, you're right, Kindred-Spirit," said Elton, "those are not the impressions we had coming into this journey. So if this is the HeartLand on this side of heaven above, why *are* there terrifying creatures here?"

"Great question my young disciple. The HeartLand is the place Mediator promised you'll have peace, joy and hope for love, trust, respect, acceptance and open heart sharing within relationships according to *His* purpose. So many resort back to creating a community for soulish purposes here on earth, resorting to the world's performance-based system, rather than walking in *Victory* by the Spirit!"

"Oh, you mean Comforter," Elton said with confidence.

"Exactly," Kindred-Spirit confirmed.

"But now that we're walking in the light with the help of Comforter, why do we tend to do that? Why wouldn't we immediately seek heart connections for the best quality of life?"

"Most likely, it's out of ignorance," Kindred-Spirit suggested. "You see...," as he engaged in his mentoring teaching mode, "...just as Mediator said to His disciples when He sent them out two-by-two, you are to be a witness to the world first by the way you love one another. That is the light you are meant to shine for others in this dark world. Remember this, the HeartLand is all about connecting in the light with your hearts wide open for the world to see! You must have courage and confidence to take on your enemies and overcome the Illusion of Light in front of those who come against you. Without Seekers like you having a passion to share the good news—especially now that you've been equipped in your heart—the rest of the Commoners will remain clueless in Suburb of Soul and never find out the truth about True Identity! You are to re-witness to Commoners by showing them the Fair Exchange, no matter how deceived they are within the performance-based system."

~

Elton and Elaine gave some serious consideration to what their mentoring Connector was saying. Even though it seemed like a very unconventional approach, they were beginning to see how their skills for combat had been developing all along the way. They were now in a spiritual war zone not only for themselves—but for other Seekers as well.

As long as Kindred-Spirit was there for them on their journey, their willingness to comply grew stronger and stronger each day. They thought of a good plan as their Inner Longings passionately drove them closer to conquering the terrifying creature—Loneliness.

"Don't buy into all that crap. I'm not going anywhere," said Loneliness. "I will always be with you wherever you go as long as you remain here on earth."

"We are not only convinced we need to get past you, we need to destroy you. You're toast sucker!" A feistier side of Elaine sprung from within.

"I'm sure you do. Everyone thinks they need to do that. In fact, I dare you to try and do that to me. But the truth of the matter is that your convictions don't matter one tiny bit to me," Loneliness said with dark coldness.

Elton tried to think of a way to get around the creature but Kindred-Spirit wouldn't let him. "Listen to your partner, Elton. You have to face Loneliness head on with the weapons in your arsenal through a joint effort if you are to pass and move forward,"

Together Elton and Elaine yielded their wills and cried out with faith from their hearts, "Mediator, please help us. We need your power, and I command your strength to give us the courage to fight this battle against Loneliness together."

And Mediator did help them. Up from the abundance of life within, the Comforter gave them the words to utter with wisdom from the Manual For Life spoken through their lips.

As they spit out truth at Loneliness, Elton and Elaine held each other tightly and stood their ground—their hearts connected as one. Finally, with a basic understanding of their Fair Exchange, each endured and overcame Loneliness by connecting their hearts. Eventually the terrifying creature disintegrated into oblivion.

And with every new milestone they sensed Mediator's favor toward them.

A great victory cry rang out among the hills throughout the land as their reputation preceded them. After that terrifying creature found his defeat, Elton and Elaine never doubted again they were Combat Soldiers!

~

As they continued throughout the HeartLand, they encountered more terrifying creatures. Some, like Money Problems opposed them with a fierce battle. There were others like Gossip, Abandonment, Disapproval, and Unfaithful Friends that tried to attack their character—inflicting wounds with harsh words. And of course, the worst of all was still yet to come, Rejection!

Very far and few in between, they were able to meet with other Seekers in homes developing a support system within a community of fellowship. As they assembled during times of rest, it was so encouraging to get built up by each other's life stories about Mediator's good work in one another. And, of course, they grew in their new knowledge and understanding of the Exchanged For Life principles without all the rhetoric and programs from the performance-based system back at their Local Gathering.

From Kindred-Spirit's wise counsel and teaching as a Connector, Elton and Elaine were seeing the bigger picture. They wished everyone could have what they embraced by faith in Mediator according to the Manual For Life. And yet, for them as a couple, every terrifying creature was one more lesson learned through the teachings about Exchanged For Life discipleship.

Their travels took them far and near to places they'd grown to love. Due to the heart connection with each other and other Seekers, their passion to fight grew stronger and stronger. One day, Elton and Elaine came across a deeply wounded soldier lying near a building called All Soul's Community Fellowship.

Elaine knelt down and held this wounded soldier in her arms and asked, "How can I help you?"

"I'm not sure you can," she said. "The Manual For Life warned us about subtleties spoken in places like that. After a while, their words became harsh, like the thrust of a sword. I got caught up in an argument with a fool and his words cut me deep. My body's getting cold, and I think my time is just about over. But whatever you do, don't go into that building! We failed to test the spirits before fellowshipping with those false teachers with false visions. They disguised their lies with half truths and tricked us with pseudo grace. When we were weary and vulnerable from the battles, those imposters took advantage of us—they are nothing more than amateur providences and they stole our affection from Mediator."

~

Like an epidemic, one by one, Elton and Elaine saw more Seekers lying help-less around the path near the All Souls Community Fellowship, deeply wounded and dying. It broke their hearts to see so many defeated believers. This wasn't supposed to happen in the HeartLand, they thought. Why would Mediator allow this? But they'd come so far and there was no turning back from pursuing their Big Dreams of their Inner Longing's.

It was getting dark as they could barely see the light of the sun reflected in the evening sky. Nearing her final hour, the wounded Combat Soldier grew weaker as Elaine could feel frailty resting heavier in her arms. Through her quivering lips, the dying soldier said, "Tell me about the meaning and purpose of your Big Dream."

After Elaine shared her amazing gifts, talents, and abilities she received from Mediator, the wounded warrior laid still for a few minutes. Then she said, "Those are some of my meaning and purpose, too. Only, my partner and I fought the most terrifying creature of them all… Rejection. He cunningly separated us over issues regarding our children. Jumping back onto the treadmill, this time, we performed deeds of Self-righteousness. Through distortions about manliness, Rejector subtly captivated my husband who began to become passive toward me again. Then he was drawn by the illusion of light for false fellowship. Then through a youth pro-gram for our kids. Even though I tried to share my heart with him, I was too late as he hardened a wall of protection embracing the illusion of light. Then, out of dis-obedience, we completely lost our heart connection, then True Identity, and finally our Passions of the Heart faded away. That's when the stronghold of disbelief solidified the wall around our hearts, and we lost our vision for our Big Dream. We could no longer hear the voice of Mediator." Then, she said one last thing to Elaine while looking intently into her fading eyes, "If you are planning to have children, be sure that you and your partner embrace the Fair Exchange together. Always maintain a heart connection wide open... and in order to overcome the illusion of light, you must get past the most terrifying creature... together!"

Elaine placed her hand to her stomach knowing there was a precious child preparing to arrive in the near future. She was waiting for just the right moment to break the news to her husband.

And with that, the wounded warrior smiled taking her last breath.

For hours, they mourned the loss of each fallen Combat Soldier.

~

The next morning, all three sat on top of a hill for a long time in silence, remembering each one's fight for freedom. Through valiant efforts, the terrifying creature was weakened. None of this was in vain. Still, the fact that it happened at all confused Elton and Elaine.

"How can this be, Kindred-Spirit?" Elaine asked.

"You are about to find out," the Connector said. "Just up ahead is your turn to take on the mega monster of them all. His name is Rejector. He is the inventor of the performance-based system."

"Forgive me for my ignorance, but I thought we already got off the tread-mill of performance through grace-based acceptance. Who is Rejector, anyway?" Elaine was almost afraid to ask.

"Well, Elaine, Rejector is the engineer of the Moral Matrix, which is the faulty system. He has multiple levels within the matrix for every whim of doctrine taught about the Manual For Life," Kindred-Spirit said in anguish. "I've seen many overconfident Seekers get plugged right back into the faulty system through its mesmerizing clutches when trying to take on this terrifying creature with very little success. But it can be done."

"How?" Elton asked.

"You will need to maintain a heart connection through the Fair Exchange with each other, endure many long hard battles that will attempt to wear you out and disconnect your hearts over time. Worst of all, he knows your thoughts and values, especially in your immediate family. That is why you are to put on the full armor of Mediator every day, in every battle. No matter how much he's capable of planting seeds of thought in an unguarded mind, he cannot read or plant thoughts when you wear the helmet of salvation and the breastplate of righteousness. Through hollow threats, you will be tempted to fight him in your own strength. He is amazing at how he can get you to spiritualize your flesh by the illusion of light."

"What! How in the world can he do that?" Elton asked.

"Trust me, he is good at getting you to engage with a soulish sympathy for children as well as your family and friends by guilting you into doing the 'right thing.' At first, he will attempt to draw you in through all kinds of flattering accolades and kudos about Self-righteous deeds in order to get you back into your flesh. Cunningly, with a very subtle means of seduction, your Self-righteousness will lead to disobedience by taking on arguments not meant for you to contend with fools. Eventually, Self-doubt sets in, exposing your disbelief… and then you will be tempted once again to protect your heart with a wall of protection rather than the full armor of Mediator."

"That will never happen to us!" Elton shouted with anger.

"We'll see, my dear friend, we'll see…," Kindred-Spirit said under his breath. Then he said directly to his young friends, "But he is relentless, and will challenge every fiber of your being when it comes to your Exchanged For Life beliefs, especially within your need for community." Then Kindred-spirit stood to his feet. "Ok, in order to prepare you with weapons for battle, you must have a ready defense gathered from the Manual For Life. Let's go back to the house and role play. Be thinking about any of the tough questions you may want to ask me that might have already come your way. Take about an hour to write down in your Journey Journals, and let's meet after lunch."

Elton and Elaine did just that.

~

After the hour had passed, Elton and Elaine reconvened with Kindred-Spirit back at his place.

"Listen," Connector began, "I understand that your Identity in Mediator has grown beyond you could have ever imagined. Perhaps we need to begin with your values and beliefs. Despite all your mixed up feelings and confused thoughts, let's get down to business and be brutally honest. Like the man who said to Mediator, *"I know what I believe, help me in my unbelief,"* let's address some questions that pertain to how your faith has at times failed you?"

"Ok, I've got one," Elaine spoke up. "I'm confused about grace ... especially when I've been taught my whole life at Local Gathering that grace is about salvation. Can you explain what it means to walk by grace?"

"Great question," as Connector leaned back crackling in his leather chair, "well, I believe according to the Manual For Life the term grace in the original Greek simply means unearned favor, or getting what we don't deserve. Yes, that's what we all get at salvation. But it's so much more than salvation. Grace allows us to live the life none of us deserve or do anything to earn. You'll be happy to know, through the years there have been numerous other believers who've blazed the same trail and described walking by grace with other terms such as: The Exchanged Life (Hudson Taylor, Charles Solomon), Walking in the Light (Ray Stedman, Chuck Swindoll), The Abiding Life (Andrew Murray), The Crucified Life (L. E. Maxwell), The Calvary Road (Roy Hesson), Freedom in Christ (Neal

Anderson), Life on the Highest Plane (Ruth Paxson), The Interior Life (Hannah Whitall Smith), The Normal Christian Life (Watchman Nee), The Victorious Christian Life (Alan Redpath, Major Ian Thomas, Bill & Anabel Gillham), and The Miracle Life (David Needham), just to name a handful," as he sat up, leaning forward.

Elton piped in, "Sir, in light of grace, I've spent practically my entire life asking a lot of *doing* questions. But I still don't fully understand how we're supposed to live Victoriously—with a capital "V"—on this side of heaven when we're such feeble, wishy-washy people battling with depravity in our flesh?"

"Excellent question my dear friend!" Connector said. "I'm right on track with you. You see, if you search for clues to the spiritual mystery of the Manual For Life, the key question to Victory is found only in the Exchanged Life. Remember when Mediator asked his own disciples, '*What can a person give in exchange for his or her soul?*' Perhaps, the life changing truth for every believer lies in acknowledging first that you cannot live the new life in and of your own abilities through your mind and emotions of the soul. Therefore, in answer to His question, there is absolutely nothing you can give in exchange for your soul. The Life Exchanger requires you to give your spirit-life in exchange for eternal life. When Comforter is sent by Mediator to exchange the dead spiritual nature of your heart, he then replaces it with a brand new pure heart, by his grace through your faith born of the Spirit.

"Ok," Elaine added with skepticism, "Remember Brother Delegator? Well, he said the teaching of grace in Exchanged For Life principles lead believers to passivity. Is it true that we can just be passive in grace?"

"Ahhh... pretty typical, and probably one of the most common arguments about walking by grace is that it teaches passivity in the life of the believer. But you can understand why, right? Commoners choosing to live in the performance-based system hate anything about grace that liberates believers to freedom from control. Passivity. Huh... nothing could be farther from the truth, my young friend.

Let me explain a little further. The grace-walk is a pro-active lifestyle empowered not by the energy of the believers own control, but by the empowerment of the indwelling life of Comforter. Our heavenly advocate, or lawyer, is Mediator Himself. He didn't just come to our defense by giving us a down-payment and we have to pay the rest off. Certainly not! He paid our penalty in full and made us complete, holy and without blame before The Life Exchanger. According to His Manual For Life, consider the example of the apostle Paul. Paul trusted Mediator to live His life through him, while leading an extremely active lifestyle according to his faith in Mediator's grace. Notice Paul's description of his lifestyle, '*And for this purpose also I labor, striving according to His power, which mightily works within me.*' Furthermore, Paul was not passive; he was active because Mediator's Comforter is active and alive. For instance, the words "labor" and "striving" in the original language refer to weariness to the point of physical exhaustion. Yet it was not done in the energy of the flesh, it was "according to His power," which was at work within Paul."

"De-e-ear Lord," Elton squeaked with a broken tone to his voice, "that's really a great way to explain grace. I wish I would have thought of that when we were arguing with Brother Delegator. We tried to explain to him it's about letting Mediator live through us. But he was pretty adamant arguing against walking by grace in the Exchanged For Life principles. He said we still have to keep all of the commandments written in Scripture and how I'm supposed to be accountable to him."

"Wow! Yeah, he's good at twisting the Manual For Life like a politician spinning legislation. Listen to me, this is not a new modern concern among those who heavily emphasize depravity of man after salvation. Just remember, in no way at all do I believe grace is a door mat to wipe our feet in passivity when we're supposed to be taking responsibility for our own Self first. In fact, this was the very essence of concern for those in the apostle Paul's own day who asked, *can we continue sinning that grace might increase*? ...to which he emphatically answered, no way! Grace enables us to freely walk in a spirit of obedience to all of Mediator's commands. And grace moves us toward righteous living due to having been made the righteousness of Mediator as a slave unto righteousness, no longer a slave unto sin. In fact, Grace overpowers sin so that you can have confidence to live according to your new righteous nature as one who's overcome the world. When grace liberates us to freedom... rules, regulations, and rigorous spiritual disciplines will not keep us from sin, rather, an authentic love relationship with Mediator will. He no longer holds our sin against us."

"That sounds good," Elaine jumped in again, "but what about where the Manual For Life says, '*if we confess our sin, The Life Exchanger is faithful to forgive us.*' Brother Delegator loves to quote that one. He says the Life Exchanger won't even talk to us or hear us talk to Him unless we confess and repent first. I've heard him say so many times that we have to confess each and every one of our sins in detail in order to be forgiven."

"Wow! I know it's hard to understand why there are so many ministers of the faith who use that verse as a means for manipulation—all that fear, shame, guilt, and pain from the performance-based system. Please take note: this is definitely one of the most common misconceptions taught in Local Gatherings today. They tell us that we have to continually confess our sins in order to be forgiven. When you take a closer look into the text, this belief is contrary to the plain teachings of the Manual For Life."

"So we don't have to confess our sins anymore?" Elton asked.

"Hmmm... I see where you're going with that. Elton, listen, I believe we've always been commanded to confess according to the real meaning of that word. Most Commoners are not taught correctly how the Life Exchanger has always required us to confess to Him. So, please understand what I'm saying. Would I ever say that confession is not important? Absolutely not!" Kindred-Spirit said matter-of-factly.

"Whew," Both Elton and Elaine sighed a sense of relief. "So, you are for confession, not against it?

"Exactly. I do *not* take a stand against confession, rather I am for what we are taught in the Manual For Life. It says believers should confess their sins, right? However, I believe that the correct teaching of confession needs to be properly understood. Check this out, *confess* is from the Greek word *homolegeo* that literally means 'same word.' It should be commonly translated as 'to say the same thing in agreement.' We are told that confessing is not only good between us and The Life Exchanger, but we are to confess one to one another because it is good for our soul. When we confess our sins to each other, we are agreeing with Mediator that we have chosen to live disobediently to His standard according to His divine revelation. Therefore, confession is not coming to each other or Mediator saying, 'Oh Lord, I have sinned, I am a dirty, rotten, no-good sinner who's heart is wretched, deceitful and desperately wicked in all it's ways, please forgive me just one more time.' But according to the Manual For Life, true confession is like this, 'I agree with Mediator's standard that I have chosen to walk in my flesh which sinned against His standard because nothing good can ever come from the flesh. Thank you Mediator that I can come boldly by your blood, which has washed my heart white as snow, because I am already forgiven by the Life Exchanger, always in past tense. I ask You, Mediator, to open my eyes to the reality of fellowship I truly have in You by your gracious acceptance of me."

Elton and Elaine sat in complete silence. Connector's words rang true to their spirit in total agreement.

"Ok you two," Kindred-Spirit continued, "it is imperative to understand that confession is primarily for us in our relationships as a reminder of Mediator's truth and promises about making us free! And then, when an individual believes in Mediator with his or her heart, they are totally forgiven (always in the past tense) of all sins past, present, and future. I personally was so amazed when I learned that the word *forgiven* used in the Greek is *Tetelestai*—meaning it is finished, paid in full." *'He made you alive together with Him, having forgiven us all our transgressions.'* Therefore, can you see that His forgiveness is not a conditional promise?"

"Yeah...," they both said in unison.

"Listen, you two, you do not have to keep on confessing in the present your sins that are committed in your fleshly performance in order to be forgiven by each other or by Mediator. As believers, we abide in Mediator's forgiveness that has already been given to us and should continuously pick up our pail, go to the well, and receive what has already been made available in the past! Did you get that? It's in the P A S T. Listen, literally in the text, when you do word studies in the proper grammar, the phrase "to forgive" is *hina aphei* in the Greek, and is in what's called a second aorist subjunctive, indicating a single act in the *past* with continual ongoing results. It's not a process in the works. When we believe on Mediator at the moment of salvation, we are forever forgiven and brought to complete restoration for all eternity. Hallelujah! Confession is granted to us through the grace of Mediator's provision. And let me also say this, consider the following translation of that passage, *'As we agree with Mediator and each other that when we sin, He reminds us that He is faithful and righteous (even when we're not) already having forgiven us of all our sins and He continually keeps us cleansed from all unrighteousness.'* Also consider this, *'...that Mediator may grant them (us) repentance leading to the knowledge of the truth.'* That is my prayer for the two of you, right now. That you will receive what He has granted you so that it will lead to a deeper knowledge of Truth."

"Well," Elaine was still in complete awe, "then what do you say to those who quote Mediator when He said in His prayer that if we forgive others then Mediator will forgive us," she inquired. "That seems conditional. How can you reconcile that with the unconditional nature of grace you're talking about?

"Well put, my friend. And I know where most go with this... 'if you don't forgive others then Father won't forgive you,' right?"

"Yes! That's exactly what I've been told," Elaine could hardly believe the accuracy of her Connector's insights.

"Well, in no way shape or form do I believe Mediator's Love Letter contradicts itself. Do you?"

"No. I don't either. But that's why I'm so confused."

"So, like you said, Mediator's prayer (or better, the model prayer) is spoken at what time?"

"What do you mean, I'm not sure what you're asking?"

"Well, notice, in that part of the Manual For Life it appears like Mediator teaches those around Him that they will be forgiven only as they forgive others. At first, this would seem to contradict the unconditional nature of love and grace as well as the forgiveness we've been talking about. I truly believe the solution lies in considering when Mediator ministered the redemptive plan of The Life Exchanger. What I mean is that He ministered his whole earthly life under those practicing the letter of the Law. He said, '*Do not think that I came to abolish the Law or the Prophets; I did not come to abolish, but to fulfill.*' As you've heard and read, during Mediators earthly ministry He and all His followers functioned under the Old Covenant of the Law. It is important to distinguish that He did not break the Law, He fulfilled the Law at a time when that was the performance-based system at its peak. In fact, the New Covenant wasn't actually initiated until the death of Mediator on the Cross, His resurrection from the grave, and then His ascension into heaven—ushering down the descension of Comforter into the hearts of every Believer as the new covenant. Therefore, our way of relating to Mediator is based on the changes after the Cross and the initiation of the grace-based gospel. So, the believer on this side of the Cross is totally forgiven (past, present, and future) at the time of salvation."

"That's amazing. I can't believe it. My whole life growing up in our Local Gathering, and I've never been told that wonderful explanation once before," Elaine said with tears in her eyes. "That would have helped comfort me so many times in the past when I felt so condemned by my performance. Instead, I did exactly what you said, I built a wall around all my fear, shame, guilt and pain to protect me from all the condemnation I felt from everyone who judged my thoughts and attitudes. Umm... if you don't mind, I have another question about our situation. When it comes to really knowing true love in our hearts, how can we explain something so subjective as... or maybe, what does it mean to comprehend the love, grace and forgiveness of Mediator in the believers heart when we have a wall of protection?"

"Oh my dear friends, the fullness of the grace of Mediator for relationships connected in the spirit cannot be understood apart from a revelation from Comforter. In all the past teachings and studying of the Manual For Life, do you recall the encouraging prayer of the apostle Paul in Ephesians 3 when he prayed, *'...that you may know the love of Mediator that surpasses knowledge.'* Recall some of the most profound words Mediator spoke, *'At that very time He rejoiced greatly in the Comforter, and said, 'I praise You, The Life Exchanger, Lord of heaven and earth, that You hid these things from the wise and intelligent and revealed them to babes. Yes, The Life Exchanger, for it was well-pleasing in Your sight. All things have been handed over to Me by You, and no one knows who the Son is except The Life Exchanger, and who The Life Exchanger is except the Son, and anyone to whom the Son wills to reveal Him.'* Isn't it wonderful that Mediator wills for all people to know Him? But get this, then Mediator said these words about Himself, *'For the Life Exchanger loves the Son and shows Him all He does.'* So, my friends, we can only come to comprehend spiritual truth as The Life Exchanger, Mediator, and Comforter reveal it to us. Revelation is a spiritual apprehension of truth. The Life Exchanger pours out His grace to us as we humbly seek Him.

"On another note," Elton interjected, "speaking of the law, I've also heard it said that walking by a wrong understanding of grace leads to a lawless attitude in the believer's life. What would you say to that?"

"Yeah, I know where that's coming from. Do not forget this because Rejector will spit this out at you just at the right time. The simple answer to this is 'No way!' The true Believer who is walking in grace is not an antinomian."

"A what! What in the world is that?" Elton asked in exasperation.

"That's one who opposes the Law. Rather, the person who is walking in grace has great respect for The Life Exchanger's sovereign purpose of the spirit of the Law. Paul the apostle said, *'So then, the Law is holy, and the commandment is holy and righteous and good.'* Grace-based believers are never to be 'Law-bashers.' But, they do understand that the legalistic letter of the Law has no place in the life of a Seeker and Thriver. Consider the following passages from the Manual For Life: *'Therefore, my brethren, you also were made to die to the Law through the body of Mediator, that you might be joined to another, to Him who was raised from the dead, that we might bear fruit for Mediator.'* *'In order that the Law might be fulfilled in us, who do not walk according to the flesh, but according to the Spirit.'* *'Realizing the fact that law is not made for a righteous man, but for those who are lawless and rebellious.'* I guarantee you've had to face that issue a lot among legalistic believers that are called Law-Conformers."

"I'm pretty sure I know this one already, but explain what is the function of the Law in the world today?" Elton inquired.

"Alright, why don't you answer and I will listen to you," Connector said as he leaned back in his leather chair.

"Well, my best explanation is that those who say there is no purpose for the Law of Mediator in the world today do not understand the plain teaching of the Manual For Life. I believe The Life Exchanger uses the Law today to cause unbelievers to realize that they are sinners in need of a Savior. I would turn to these passages: *'Because by the works of the Law no flesh will be justified in His sight; for through the Law comes the knowledge of sin.'* *'And the Law came that the transgression might increase; but where sin increased, grace abounded all the more.'* *'Therefore the Law has become our tutor to lead us to Mediator, that we may be justified by faith.' 'The sting of death is sin, and the power of sin is the law.'* *'For whoever keeps the whole law and yet stumbles in one point, he has become guilty of all.'* So, basically, from these verses I believe the Law has a definite purpose in the world today, but not legalistically in the lives' of believers."

"Good job buddy! What about you Elaine. You've been awfully quiet."

"Oh, I'm just taking down notes and listening for now. But I do have a question about a word you used. What exactly is Legalism?"

"I thought you might ask that. Well, I define legalism as rules with a system of performance-based living in which a person tries to make spiritual progress in order to gain Mediator's and other's acceptance and favor based on what they *do*. Perhaps, in other words, Legalism is focused on the believers behavior. It is therefore an achieving system for grace. And yet, consequently, if you really consider what that means, Legalism is the opposite of grace. The Manual For Life tells us that Mediator's grace is a system of living where The Life Exchanger blesses us because we are in His Son, Mediator, and for no other reason at all. Grace is focused on our spiritual birthright and is therefore a receiving system. Here's some more good passages from the Manual For Life: *'Mediator redeemed us from the curse of the Law, having become a curse for us.'* *'For the grace of Mediator has appeared, bringing salvation to all men, instructing us to deny worldly desires and to live sensibly, righteously in the present age.'"*

Elaine stepped back up to the plate in full swing, "So does walking in grace according to the spirit of the Law imply that a believer never needs the Law to point out our sin and that we never sin anymore?"

Kindred-spirit leaned forward toward her, "Gooood, my young disciple. You'll need this one for sure. Listen, nowhere does the Manual For Life say or imply that a believer is sinlessly perfect, if that's what you're asking? Here are the words of the apostle John making this abundantly clear, *'If we say we have no sin, we are deceiving ourselves, and the truth is not in us.'* Yet, at the same time, we must understand that as believers the power of sin has been broken in our lives so that we do not have to sin. The apostle Paul says, *'Therefore do not let sin reign in your mortal body that you should obey its lusts, and do not go on presenting the members of your body to sin as instruments of unrighteousness; but present your- selves to Mediator as those alive from the dead, and your members as instruments of righteousness to Mediator.'* And please know my precious friends that this does not mean we are incapable of sin; it literally means we have a choice to either sin or not sin. But the power of sin has been broken in our lives. A careful study will reveal that although our old nature was put to death at salvation, we still have a struggle with the flesh for the rest of our journey here on earth. As you may recall, the flesh is the way we have learned to meet our needs independent of Mediator. As believers we have a choice, we can walk in the flesh or in the Spirit."

"Ok, so how can a person learn to practically abide in Mediator?"

"Great question. Wow, you both are really staying focused. I'm proud of you. Well, to answer your question, the word *abide* comes from an agricultural term when a farmer grafts a branch into the trunk of a tree or into a vine. What it means in practical terms is to continue, to remain, or to stay. Abiding occurs as we make the conscious choice to moment-by-moment rest in Mediator and allow Him to bear His fruit through us. Perhaps the classic expression of this truth is where Mediator says, *'I am the vine, you are the branches; he who abides in Me, and I in him, he bears much fruit; for apart from Me you can do nothing.'* When Mediator says *"nothing"* the Greek word means nothing of eternal worth or value. As believers, we are not called to strive or work to bear fruit for Mediator. We are called to abide or rest in Him allowing Him to produce His fruit and good works through us. We are not fruit producers we are fruit bearers."

With that, it was time for Elton and Elaine to pursue the inevitable battle with the next terrible creature.

~

Word spread quickly throughout the land, these new Combat Soldiers were about to challenge the darkest terrible creature of them all—Rejector. But first, they had to overcome the Illusion of Light.

All the wounded Seekers gathered around the arena of stronghold to watch.

Elton and Elaine walked up to Rejector very cautiously with special protection on their eyes Kindred-spirit had given them. But even with the eye protection, the Illusion of Light was still very tempting to look at.

First, they tried to negotiate, "We come to you in the name of Mediator and stand firmly on the Manual of Life, depart from here and be gone," they spoke in unison. "We claim freedom for every Seeker and Thriver in your camp. Release them from the darkness of the Illusion of Light!" they demanded.

When Rejector exploded from his position with a burst of dazzling light, all the Seekers gasped. "None of them will ever be free to overcome the performance-based system ever again. Through their despicable, desperate need for acceptance, they have disobeyed with disbelief, now they all have walls of protection around their hearts due to fear, shame, guilt, and pain, forever! They have been rejected by Mediator who will not forgive unconfessed sin. Now, they can't even hear or see the Word you proclaim because they don't have ears to hear or eyes to see. Their hope has been put off and their Inner Longings are no more. Soon they will either die or go back to Suburb of Soul in all their depravity and wretched Self-righteousness, where they will once again be accepted based only on their performance, which at this time is FAILURE!!!"

Just as Kindred-Spirit warned them, Rejector spit out the most hideous lies twisted in such unthinkable terms. Elton and Elaine fought courageously together. The Fair Exchange seemed to be working with every weapon and piece of armor they used. But after days and weeks, they grew weary.

The temptation to disobey through disbelief was not what they thought it would be. There were no blatant disregards for commands written in the Manual For Life. In fact, it was just the opposite. Like a boxer, through a false confidence to stand for their beliefs, they were growing weary from taking jab after jab. They thought they were supposed to take on any and all of the violations that were clearly opposed to the Manual of Life. They basically tried to defend Mediator's total Word as if that was their battle aim. How could that possibly be a problem of disobedience? And how could that lead to disbelief? What Elton and Elaine failed to see was that they were trying to seek favor through the appearance of good morals called deeds of Self-righteousness—that was the Illusion of Light blind them. Something the terrifying creature knew about the weakness of all human beings, and took full advantage.

They retreated. Then Elaine said to Elton, "Remember what Common Sense told us about opposition when we were up against our Crazy-Makers?"

"Yeah. He told us to turn our opposition into opportunity!" Elton replied.

"Excellent!" Kindred-Spirit exhorted. "Do you remember from the Manual For Life, there was another Combat Warrior about to lose his head in prison for taking on battles he never should have? Mediator told him that no one would fall away on *His* account?"

"That's right," Elaine said in agreement. "We can only battle each terrifying creature's issues that pertain to our passions and convictions. Elton, if we try to battle for other worthy causes that are not part of our calling, the Illusion of Light will consume us in our own Self efforts to perform deeds of Self-righteousness all over again!"

~

And that's when they overcame the temptation of the Faulty System's Illusion of Light.

Elton and Elaine regrouped.

They cried out to Mediator, "We need you to fight our battles *through* us. Are you with us?"

"Yes, I am with you always," Mediator replied.

"We are too weak," Elaine said in exhaustion

"Yes... *you* are."

"The Faulty System is too strong for us!" Elton yelled.

"Yes... *it* is."

"Show us how to *be* so we can know how to feel and think with our hearts."

"Good. You are beginning to Believe!" Mediator praised them. "The plan this time...," He explained, "...stand your ground together with your Hearts Connected in a Fair Exchange and guarded by *my* full armor. Focus with your unique Inner Longings I gave you. Put down all the weapons you've been using. Look to your Journey Journals. Write across a blank page the word GRACE! Ok, now look at what's in your hand. Take your Swiss Army knife-pens with you and the battle will be yours to bring me glory. I promise not only to be with you, but I will go before you. Wait to see my sign."

That is exactly what they chose. Sure enough, all their meaning and purpose came alive like never before. No more distractions. No more assumptions. They stood their ground on the living Manual For Life and resisted everything the terrifying creature could throw at them.

But the Seekers watching were not impressed. They were terribly disappointed.

Then, as Combat Soldiers, Elton and Elaine put down all their weapons they'd been using. They pulled out their Swiss Army knife-pens, aiming them straight toward the hideous target.

All those watching gasped in horror, which only increased their disbelief. Now, each one felt their hope slip even further away.

The terrifying creature mocked them with laughter and accusations in front of all the other Seekers, "Are you serious? You foolish Commoners with your puny little knife-pens. I know all your past issues and mistakes," listing many of them out loud to cause shame and embarrassment for everyone to hear. "Are you going to slay me with your little knives? There is nothing in the present with your puny little *Selves* you can scare me with that will overcome all the bad from your past I can destroy you with!" He roared and growled like he was the king of the world.

Elton and Elaine weren't sure what to do, now feeling pretty humiliated. Even Kindred-Spirit hid his quivering eyes behind an umbrella for a moment. But they just stood their ground and spoke more truth from the Manual For Life in the name of Mediator, "There is no more judgment and condemnation for all who put their trust in Mediator. If Mediator is for us, nothing is big enough to accuse and defeat us."

But the mega monster towered over them looking pretty impressive robed with all his Illusion of Light.

Then in unison, "Greater is He that is in us than you who is in the world!"

That was the sign to finish the negotiations. With that, Mediator sprung from within in a glorious light, disrobing the ugly monster of his illusion of light. Elton and Elaine could sense the empowerment of their knife-pens as they became weapons of mass destruction, overcoming and revealing to all the other Seekers the Illusions of the terrifying creature. All the bells and whistles became the weapon of choice none of the others had ever relied upon.

Finally, this toothless creature was exposed for what he really is, and he cowardly retreated from them leaving all the community of Seekers free from strongholds and bondage.

They all knew a miracle when they saw one.

Soon a celebration broke out. The joyful Community sang and danced with awe. But their reverence wasn't directed toward Elton and Elaine. Instead, they repented with Godly sorrow making things right on every point, restoring their belief in Mediator, and gave great thanks and adoration toward Him for their restoration unto Freedom!

~

Elton and Elaine slipped away as the crowd was a bit much for their weary souls and bodies.

Barely able to stay awake, they had used up their last bit of energy to write in their Journey Journals.

One thing for sure, they both needed a good night of sleep before the big celebration the next day.

Chapter 9 Journey Journal

Here lies the test of courage. Every believer is faced with difficulties (terrifying creatures). The greatest tendency is to fall back into a protective mode and take back control with the weapons of our soul. Yet, like Mediator before us, He lived the example of a man who never allowed his soul take control. Rather, the Spirit always took control over His soul (John chapter 5). Before we face the horror in front of us, we must count the cost. There are those who will warn us if we listen.

But who are the ones given the job to be Gate-Keepers, Good-Shepherds, and Connectors? At every healthy community fellowship, there need to be those who exemplify good character. The 3 most important characteristics to look for are: #1) Spirit-filled; #2) Humble; and #3) Well grounded in Scripture. Perhaps the issue for us is the critical need for trust.

Who do you trust? Please write down his/her name and describe your relationship with them.

_____

_____

_____

_____

The Gate-Keeper in our story showed the integrity of one who's completely loyal to Mediator. He obeyed Him above all else. Also a mentoring Connector is someone who takes a personal interest in you and walks with you along your journey.

Do you have a trustworthy mentoring Connector?   Yes or No   Take this simple test and see how they line up.

MY MENTOR/CONNECTOR _____ TAKES A PERSONAL INTEREST IN MY LIFE WHO:	NO!	No	no	yes	Yes	YES!
…is personal and knows me well at the heart level	1	2	3	4	5	6
…holds me accountable regularly (<u>once</u> a week)	1	2	3	4	5	6
…openly shares similar convictions of values & beliefs	1	2	3	4	5	6
…is a master communicator w/ knowledgeable insight	1	2	3	4	5	6
…is an active listener who really hears my heart	1	2	3	4	5	6
…takes the time to understand my (+) & (-) Traits	1	2	3	4	5	6
…has a genuine passion for life & for my well-being	1	2	3	4	5	6
…has good credentials & the utmost integrity	1	2	3	4	5	6
…has solid coaching & counseling experience	1	2	3	4	5	6
…has good insightful wisdom regarding my potential	1	2	3	4	5	6
…is safe for me to open up to without any reservations	1	2	3	4	5	6
…asks all the right questions about my specific needs	1	2	3	4	5	6
…respects & keeps confidentiality in high priority	1	2	3	4	5	6
…is trustworthy and has gained my confidence	1	2	3	4	5	6
…gives me the freedom to express my inner person	1	2	3	4	5	6
…is sincerely compassionate, upbeat, & encouraging	1	2	3	4	5	6
…validates and affirms my meaning & purpose	1	2	3	4	5	6
…gives unconditional support even when I mess up	1	2	3	4	5	6
…keeps me focused on who I am within myself	1	2	3	4	5	6
…gives a balanced biblical perspective from the inside-out	1	2	3	4	5	6
SUB TOTALS:						
GRAND TOTAL:						

God said in Genesis that it is not good that man be alone. Unfortunately, the life of a believer who is sold out and committed to following Mediator, can find his or her Self very lonely at times… to say the least. We must face Loneliness.

How do you deal with loneliness?

_____

_____

_____

_____

Like Loneliness, what other terrifying creatures can you relate to the most on your journey?

_____

_____

_____

_____

In spiritual warfare, it is very popular to emphasize overcoming the darkness. But it has been my experience and observation that most believers are not dabbling in the Ouija Board Spells, Tarot Cards, Palm Readings, or Sorcery. Instead, they not only entertain vain philosophies, but even ideologies and theologies that are presenting false doctrine. Paul talks about this in Colossians chapter 2. That's why we have to be careful of the illusion of light leading to the illusion of control.

Identify some of the illusions of light you find yourself dealing with in your life and write them down in detail.

_____

_____

_____

_____

For Elton and Elaine, their travels took them far and near to places they'd grown to love. Due to the heart connection with each other and other believers, their passions grew stronger and stronger. One day, they came across a deeply wounded soldier lying near a building called All Soul's Community Fellowship.

Personally, I have reached out to so many soldiers wounded by unhealthy churches and asked, "How can I help you?"

Most respond "I'm not sure." Yet, not many realize how adamantly the Bible warns us about subtleties spoken from bad leaders. After a while, their words become harsh, like the thrust of a sword. We get caught up in futile arguments, and their words cut us deep. Most of us fail to test the spirits before seeking fellowship with false teachers with false visions. Without true accountability, they disguise their agendas with half truths. When we grow weary and vulnerable, those imposters take advantage of us — they are nothing more than amateur providence's who steal our affection from Mediator."

In fact, as our perfect example, only one Good-Shepherd has ever lived the exchanged spirit-filled life *perfectly* — that was Mediator Himself! (1st Timothy 2:5 and Hebrews 8:6; 9:15;12:24). Plus, we are told in the book of Philippians chapter two that Mediator was accountable to the Father when He exchanged His divine attributes for a life completely relying on the Spirit. However, there is good news for us. Just like Mediator, Comforter will continue to live His *Victorious* life through us. Mediator is the author and finisher of your faith (Hebrews 12:2). Perhaps no verse in the Manual For Life says it more clearly than "*I have been crucified with Christ; and it is no longer I who live, but Christ lives in me (and through me); and the life which I now live in the body I live by faith in Him, who loved me, and delivered Himself up for me*" (Galatians 2:20).

Reflect on your journey and write down in your Journey Journal what you've learned about your identity in Mediator and how that has made a difference in the way you rely upon the Spirit to live His life through you.

_____

_____

_____

_____

Chapter 10

Building Community
With Other Believers

ime stood still in the hearts of our young pioneers. Both Elton and Elaine reflected back on their journey. Nothing seemed as it once was now that their lives embraced the Exchanged Life from the Life Exchanger. His divine intervention ("*kairos*") in time and space ("*chronos*") fulfilled His invitation with love and grace. It seemed like almost a lifetime ago. So many miles. So many lessons. So many obstacles to overcome. They were certainly exchanged for life.

"You've now made it to the Heartland my young followers." Kindred-Spirit said near a bubbling brook where Elton and Elaine were sitting.

"Yeah, we can hardly wait to go back to Suburb of Soul and share everything we learned on our journey," Elaine said with a sigh of relief.

"Yeah, me too," Elton responded glancing over at Kindred-Spirit. "But there's more, isn't there?"

"Yes, my dear friend, there's so much more that lasts beyond a lifetime here on earth."

"Will we be leaving soon to go back or will we be going on another adventure with you?" Elaine impatiently asked.

"Don't worry, precious one. In due time you will see your family and friends again. But first, we must attend a great celebration! You are two of the honored guests sitting up on the stage with me. But don't worry, you don't have to speak if you don't want to. They just want to give you recognition before the whole community. You'll see, it'll be a lot of fun full of good times for everyone."

"Can we spend the day alone? We're still pretty tired and needing some down time," Elaine asked.

"No problem. But I'd like to make a suggestion. No, actually a request of both of you. There is another very important step in your journey... then I will ask you a very important question later. There is something we call a Time Line where you put on a chart your entire journey from birth until now. It will have a significant impact from here. Let me explain..."

Kindred-Spirit drew a chart for both Elton and Elaine explaining each step to fill out and complete the task.

~

Booming with the thunderous sounds from an array of luminous fireworks, celebration filled the air. There was nothing quite like the night sky lit up in glitter with reflections of sparkling colors on the lakefront. From the panoramic view in the middle of the valley, the best seat in the house was at the end of the dock, hovering over Virtuous Lake. There, two very relieved Seekers were sitting. All around them, they could see hope in everyone's eyes. Laughter and music echoed off the hillsides surrounding every direction as the community gathered for the big Thanksgiving event in honor of Mediator's Victory.

"I'm so proud of you Elton," Elaine said, affirming her man.

"Thanks. I'm proud of you too. I could never have fought the good fight without you."

"Elton," Elaine responded staring into his eyes with that look of something special.

"Yes." Elton said sensing something was about to happen.

"I have something to tell you."

"Ok, what is it."

"Remember when we were told to pass this on to our children? Well, I believe you are going to be a wonderful follower of The Life Exchanger. One who passes on a wonderful heritage to your child."

"Yeah. I believe we're a pretty good team together and some day our kids will have a great future."

"Well," Elaine paused holding her stomach, "I'm pretty sure this one's great future will be sooner than you think."

"What!" Elton sprang to his feet. "You mean... you're serious... I mean... we're going to be parents?"

"Yep. In about seven months, you're going to be a daddy."

Just then, Kindred-Spirit joined Elton and Elaine.

"Hey, Kindred-Spirit, did you hear? I'm going to be a daddy!"

"Congratulations my friend. That's fantastic!"

Suddenly, the piercing sound of the old train whistle, the same one that blew for the early pioneers here in the HeartLand over a century ago, screamed out interrupting all the festivities to inform everyone that the announcement was about to begin. The entire community was required to attend this monumental occasion. Never before has there been such excitement with hopeful anticipation for so much potential throughout the community of believers.

Stepping up to the microphone, one of the Community Elder's started his announcement, "The fate of this community was hanging in the balance. Today, we are gathered together to announce New Beginnings for all Seekers in the HeartLand. Here, sitting behind me, are the bondservants who had the courage to believe when everyone else gave into their flesh. In front of the entire community, we'd like to ask them to stay here with us and remain a part of our Community and teach the Exchanged For Life principles with their unique gifts, talents, and abilities!"

The Community exploded in celebration with cheers.

"However, I will say up front...," the community Elder spoke with a hint of despair in his voice, as the roar of the crowd simmered. "The community Elders want all of you Seekers to know that before the celebration continues; there will be a Solemn Assembly of humble repentance on all our part. With deep sorrow and great remorse, we need to seek The Life Exchanger's forgiveness and to grant us repentance and reconciliation as we have not served you well. We humbly recognize the one with the gift of Connector, accompanied by the two Combat Soldiers; they are to be commended for their faithfulness to Mediator and the truth written in the Manual For Life. They have served well as an example to all. We will never forget their valiant efforts along with all those who fought for our freedom. We suggest to you, repent, be reconciled, and may The Life Exchanger restore us all from this day forward as we take back the promised HeartLand that was given to our forefathers before us. We are never again to return to the Faulty System of performance-based acceptance through deeds of the flesh!"

The crowd broke down in sorrow and remorse right then. There was a deep drone of moaning and groaning in postures of pain and suffering. For in their weakness, they did not know how to pray as they should, but Comforter interceded for them presenting each and every repentant heart before The Life Exchanger, expressing their groanings too deep for words. After a season of mourning, reconciliation from The Life Exchanger's mercy and grace restored favor with the presence of His peace. The celebration continued throughout the next day and the next night.

~

After the celebration was over, everyone went back to seeking The Life Exchanger for their Big Dream.

Kindred-Spirit had more lessons prepared for Elton and Elaine before they pursued the rest of their vision.

"Thank you for filling out your Life Line. Now I must ask, are you willing to embrace your vision for your Big Dream among these Seekers?" Kindred-Spirit asked Elton on a brisk walk the next morning.

"Yes, Kindred-Spirit," he replied. "Even though there are still things left undone, I'm not sure how to accomplish them."

Elton still had some reservations about his Inner Longing's Meaning and Purpose. He could envision a community where he would accomplish his Big Dream and share in the almost effortless connections with others—especially partnering in the Fair Exchange with Elaine and a future family.

As they walked among the newly released Seekers throughout the community of the HeartLand, due to his journey through the Unknown Wilderness, Elton had a whole new perspective when observing thoughts and emotions with his heart. His internal radar was now hyper sensitive to the *internal* needs, rather than gauging his choices by *external* symptoms. It became very obvious that the yoke of bondage had taken its toll on many believers souls; leaving them scarred and badly wounded. Amazingly, having accomplished the big victory over the Illusion of Light now behind them, each and every one of their spirits were lifted high beyond external conditions. But they were still missing that one key element of becoming heart connected with others in their community through the Fair Exchange.

The next day, grateful Seekers everywhere pleaded with Elton and Elaine to reconsider a permanent residence among them. With a welcome like that, who could resist?

But Elaine, especially at first, could not grasp the idea of staying among this community permanently where she would be so far removed from her family back in Suburb of Soul. Eventually, those exact same sentiments came over Elton as well. They wanted to return to their Perspective Home and join others like Best Friend and Common Sense to share all that they'd learned with everyone who would listen to their story. But there was something they were still holding on to.

~

In the days that followed, Elton walked through every street and neighborhood of the fragile community. Extending his gift of wise counsel and teaching, he helped mend the inflicted injuries with wisdom from the Manual For Life. Individuals, couples, and whole families were experiencing breakthroughs like never before due to a reconnection of their Identities with Mediator. There was a healing throughout the land among all those who were willing. Their connected-heart relationships grew in covenants of love among the community, finally making a difference beyond unrealistic expectations.

In the midst of a changing community, Mediator said, "Well done my good and faithful servants."

"Only by your grace and love," Elaine responded with a gentle smile glowing from her whole face.

"Elton," He said.

"Yes, here am I, at your service."

"What do your eyes see now?"

Elton pondered for a moment. He looked into the eyes of the adults and children around him. "I see a remnant of believers who have been badly wounded, still many with reluctant walls of protection guarding their hearts. Many of them still have a need for something they've yet to realize about their true meaning and purpose for their new identity in you. But each and every one of them has new hope due to the recent happenings."

"That is what I see too," Mediator concurred. "What else do you see?"

At that moment, Elton was standing in front of the Community Fellowship building where they assembled regularly on the first day of every week for good teaching, prayer, fellowship, and breaking bread in remembrance of Mediator. It was there that The Life Exchanger was adding new believers to their community every day. He looked up. He could hardly believe his eyes. Etched in stone around the base of the building was a story, much like his own, each and every detail read of the mysteries written in the Manual For Life. Because of the gospel of grace, they were called Grace Fellowship of HeartLand.

"Your Big Dream for your Inner Longing's is calling out to you," Mediator said.

Could it be true? Elton pondered for more than a minute over the possibilities what this might mean for his future.

Like in most other cases, Elaine was first to have a peace running through her veins causing a burst of compassion spoken through her lips, "It is true!" She yelled. "You're at the place where your meaning and purpose is confirmed that you are a Connector! You and Kindred-Spirit have a like mindedness for the same passion and vision. This is the opportunity of a lifetime!"

Astounded, Elton instantly knew it was true. He had arrived beyond all his past potential and was finally standing in the window of his present purpose—he was a Connector.

Suddenly, Elton realized why he hadn't understood his Big Dream that had been right in front of him all along. What came so naturally, he took for granted. He hadn't fully embraced the natural grace gifts Comforter gave him to find his niche in order to accomplish his Big Dream. The connection between his Big Dream and his Inner Longings was hinging on the heart connection between he and Mediator. Elton had been looking to the wrong source to validate his Meaning and Purpose, rather than cling to the one who knew him best—Mediator. The fantastic place he'd imagined all along was not his vision at all. Rather, the meaning and purpose of his Inner Longings needed a Fair Exchange with other Seekers like himself. This could only come through brokenness of Self in order to truly become thankful for his precious gifts from the Giver.

To his surprise, the *needs* of these Seekers perfectly matched his Big Dream in his Innermost Being. And now, with wisdom and understanding about his true Identity through joy and peace, Elton was prepared to accomplish his Inner Longing's according to the wisdom and strength of Comforter guiding the rest of his journey.

~

That very evening, Elton became more excited about pursuing his New Beginnings for his Inner Longing's where his passions were destined to bear fruitfulness. Needless to say, the burdens were tremendously heavy. Only, this time, he was not willing to forfeit The Life Exchanger's grace by clinging to his old methods of stinkin'-thinkin.' With the lessons he learned along his journey, Elton decided not to focus his expectations ever again on the validation of other Commoner's. Instead, with a renewed thankful heart, he was determined more than ever to offer his gifts, talents, and abilities in humble service. Mediator showed him favor because of who he is, not for what he had done or had not done. Elton also learned not to take rejection so personally from those who could not see what they were doing when they'd hurt him. His prayer became, "Forgive them, for they know not what they are doing."

Elton had no idea where to begin the process but he had a vision to simply begin. Along each new path, the worries of Money Problems were still terrifying. Loneliness would try and creep up among the old guards standing their ground. The ever present fear of rejection from unfaithful friends, as well as the Illusions of Light from Self-righteousness, all competed for his affections to meet his needs independent of The Life Exchanger. That is why he had to die to Self daily.

Elton remained steadfast and true.

The one advantage he now had, which towered over any terrifying creatures, was his Fair Exchange with Elaine as long as his heart remained wide open and connected—and absent of any walls. As a renewed believer, his steadfast faithfulness to following the Manual For Life also required a constant clinging to Comforter with his heart yielded, daily.

Elton reached out to those nearest him first. Willing to offer what he had, he spent everything he had, only according to his means, knowing never to get into the bondage of debt ever again.

His new motto to live by was, NGOG—No Guilt Only Grace."

Time passed, and he worked hard. Accomplishing his Big Dream's Inner Longings was challenging at times, but Elton had never known such sweet fulfillment before. He watched The Life Exchanger rebuild something wonderful out of what had been broken, and made it better than ever before. Elton was supplying big demands while wisely accomplishing what he loved most from the Passions of his Heart. He no longer held on to his Big Dream or Inner Longing's as his *baby*.

One day Kindred-Spirit strategized a plan with Elton. They walked together and talked together helping many young and old believers along the way. Then Kindred-Spirit inquired more about Elton's accomplishments.

Elton's renewed spirit and recent accomplishments spoke volumes of growth and maturity.

Immediately, the Elders and leaders of Grace Fellowship saw that it was true. This once ordinary Commoner, was now equipped with the Fair Exchange and displayed extraordinary gifts, talents, and abilities they themselves lacked in the area of building heart connected relationships. Elton had also acquired skills for networking connections they'd never considered before. He was meeting important needs that most Elders couldn't. Instead of becoming threatened, these wise Elders knew this was a spiritual synergy from The Life Exchanger that they were to share in a collaborative effort for the good of the whole community.

This was a very joyful time for Elton, and a very good day for the community at Grace Fellowship.

~

More time passed. Elton was devoted to handing out helpful gifts as the community discovered more about the Exchanged For Life principles. He put together a website everyone could rely upon for more information about their very own unique Inner Longings. Elton was very careful to remain completely dependant upon Comforter in order to remain in Mediator and only speak what was in his spirit. He also continued faithfully, never compromising or taking for granted what had been given to him as a precious gift—Elaine.

Then one day, he made another important discovery.

He approached a group of believers who had a problem with their new Identities. The more their urges grew about who they're meant to *be*, the more they grew confused about what they were supposed to *do*! Elton noticed new contentions growing around their hearts as they complained among each other, just like he remembered about Mediator recorded in the Manual For Life.

He asked them, "Who do you believe you really are in Mediator? Do you understand the meaning of Mediator living through you? And what is the meaning and purpose of your Big Dream?"

When they gave their best efforts to answer, Elton immediately recognized the problem. He wisely remembered that every *quest* begins with asking the right *questions*. So he took an assessment of each one.

"Have any of the previous Connectors ever walked you through Exchanged For Life discipleship?

"No," they all replied.

"Hmmm... I know exactly what you need!" Elton spoke again with confidence. "Here's how I can help you."

~

On a particular event, all the Seekers, including the Elders, gathered as a Community at the Grace Fellowship building. Elton put together a presentation tailored just for them. He knew exactly what was missing. So he and Elaine began sharing their teachings about the Exchanged For Life discipleship.

It was a wonderful message beginning with discipleship, helping so many believers overcome their Self-centered lives in the Flesh, and about their Inner Longings for true Identity. And coupled with the need for heart connections through the Fair Exchange, of course, are passions for their Big Dream. Each session held jewels of wisdom addressing restoration in search of their Inner Longings—learning to surrender their soul's control in order to live according to the control of the Spirit. It included the need for Brokenness in order to experience Wholeness, which always leads to Fruitfulness, and finally Connectedness

Most importantly, it was a message of grace about allowing Mediator to live *through* them.

As time progressed, the HeartLand community took back the vision of the early pioneers. The Seekers of Grace Fellowship began to fit the vision of Elton's Big Dream. More and more, the HeartLand was filled with believers experiencing New Beginnings by becoming Exchanged For Life.

Then one day Mediator said, "There's more."

"More?" Elton repeated.

"Yes, there's so much more. Are you willing to trust me?"

"I trust you with every fiber of my being."

"Your name is no longer Elton. You and your wife are to be called Thriver and Intuition from now on. And one other thing... you *are* a Connector. So shepherd my sheep and lead well, my good and faithful servant."

And in that moment, Thriver understood. No matter how he thought or felt about what was happening right then, he was to never fill in the blank and write the end of his story. He was to always be prepared and willing when The Life Exchanger would say, "Come, follow me..."

Chapter 10 Journey Journal

What a journey it's been! The following 2 charts are to help you see Elton's Time Line. Next, fill in your own chart on the next page. Use this outline chronologically across the middle gauging +1 to +10 on top and -1 to -10 on bottom identifying your positive and negative experiences. (Note each of the different stages of your life along the middle line.)

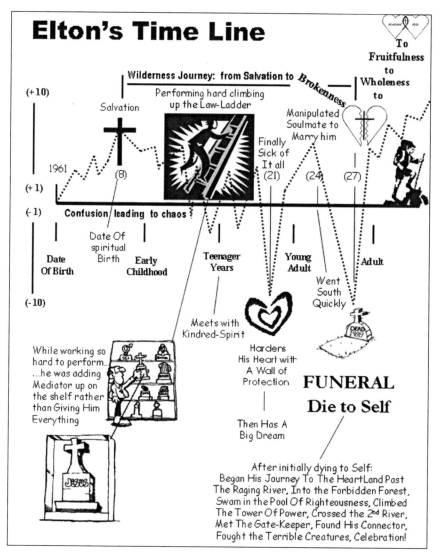

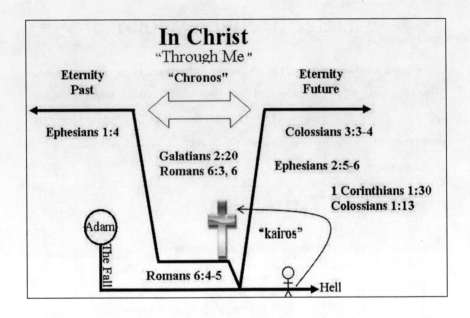

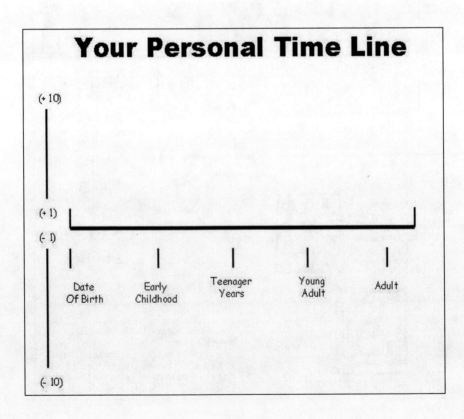

In summary, we've learned about: 1) Discipleship, 2) our true Identity in Christ, 3) New Beginnings, 4) who we *were* in Adam vs. who *we* are in Christ, 5) viewing our Self from an Inside-out perspective, 6) live as Spirit-filled Tri-part beings, and 7) deny our Self daily and carry our cross (the Tree of Life) baring fruit of righteousness. Finally, the Exchanged For Life experience should be reflected in how we connect our new hearts in relationships as Connectors. The greatest evangelical verse comes from the words of Mediator: *"By this all men will know that you are My disciples, if you have love (agape) for one another."* Jn. 13:35. So, we should be *different* as children of light making a *difference* in a world of darkness. Love well!

Before moving forward with your vision for your Big Dream, remember that your life is an intricate part of something God began a long time ago. You have a heritage in Christ that God was passing on through His original community of believers. I'd like to leave you with a passage of Scripture declaring the Word of The Life Exchanger to all of His people:

Here's what he said, "So it shall be when all of these things have come upon you, the blessing and the curse which I have set before you, and you call them to mind in all nations where the LORD your God has banished you, and you return to the LORD your God and obey Him with all your heart and soul according to all that I command you today, you and your sons, then the LORD your God will restore you from captivity, and have compassion on you, and will gather you again from all the peoples where the LORD your God has scattered you. "If your outcasts are at the ends of the earth, from there the LORD your God will gather you, and from there He will bring you back. "The LORD your God will bring you into the land which your fathers possessed, and you shall possess it; and He will prosper you and multiply you more than your fathers. "Moreover the LORD your God will circumcise your heart and the heart of your descendants, to love the LORD your God with all your heart and with all your soul, so that you may live. "The LORD your God will inflict all these curses on your enemies and on those who hate you, who persecuted you. "And you shall again obey the LORD, and observe all His commandments which I command you today. "Then the LORD your God will prosper you abundantly in all the work of your hand, in the offspring of your body and in the offspring of your cattle and in the produce of your ground, for the LORD will again rejoice over you for good, just as He rejoiced over your fathers; if you obey the LORD your God to keep His commandments and His statutes which are written in this book of the law, if you turn to the LORD your God with all your heart and soul. "For this commandment which I command you today is not too difficult for you, nor is it out of reach. "It is not in heaven, that you should say, 'Who will go up to heaven for us to get it for us and make us hear it, that we may observe it?' "Nor is it beyond the sea, that you should say, 'Who will cross the sea for us to get it for us and make us hear it, that we may observe it?' "But the word is very near you, in your mouth and in your heart, that you may observe it. "See, I have set before you today life and prosperity, and death and adversity; in that I command you today to love the LORD your God, to walk in His ways and to keep His commandments and His statutes and His judgments, that you may live and multiply, and that the LORD your God may bless you in the land where you are entering to possess it. "But if your heart turns away and you will not obey, but are drawn away and worship other gods and serve them, I declare to you today that you shall surely perish. You will not prolong your days in the land where you are crossing the Jordan to enter and possess it. "I call heaven and earth to witness against you today, that I have set before you life and death, the blessing and the curse. So choose life in order that you may live, you and your descendants, by loving the LORD your God, by obeying His voice, and by holding fast to Him; for this is your life and the length of your days, that you may live in the land which the LORD swore to your fathers, to Abraham, Isaac, and Jacob, to give them." (Deuteronomy 30)

Love, The Life Exchanger, Mediator, Comforter

LaVergne, TN USA
25 September 2010
198446LV00002B/2/P